"Terry Whalin has written an informative book to help people navigate the treacherous waters of getting published. An indispensable tool for new authors."
—**Scott Waxman**, Literary Agent and President of the Waxman Agency

"In the often bewildering world of book publishing, aspiring authors need more than desire, creative skill, and something worthwhile to say. They also need a road map. My friend Terry Whalin offers a map even Rand-McNally couldn't top. If you have any inclination toward getting a book published, you'll do well by studying this book first."
—**Larry Libby**, Senior Editor, Multnomah Publishers

"This is a valuable step-by-step guide to doing a book proposal. It tells would-be authors what agents and editors look for in book proposals, with advice on how you can tailor your book proposal for the market at which you're aiming."
—**Timothy Harper**, editor, The ASJA Guide to Freelance Writing

"How does one get a foot in the editorial door? Publishers want to see a clear, direct, and well organized book proposal. Without one, most will not get a second chance to make a good first impression. Terry Whalin's excellent how-to advice in *Book Proposals That Sell* will be of immense value to nonfiction writers of all types."
—**Leonard G. Goss**, Editorial Director, Broadman & Holman Publishers

"Writers who are serious about getting published need more than talent. They need the inside scoop on what really goes on in publishing. Terry Whalin offers insider information for writers at every level in *Book Proposals That Sell*. This book is bursting with real life examples and bottom-line advise to create professional proposals that will make editors sit up and take notice."
—**Vicki Caruana**, teacher and author of the bestselling *Apples & Chalkdust.*

"Terry Whalin has written scor   acquisitions editor at two publishing l   propos-als. Now he shares his wealth   brim-ming with pointers."
—**Janet Kobobel Grant**, Litera

"Traditional publishing is shrouded with mystery. Terry Whalin peels back the curtain to give authors an inside look at what a writer needs to provide a publisher. Following his advice will give you the edge you need to create a slam dunk proposal!"

—**Michael S. Hyatt**, President of Thomas Nelson Publishers

"As a former publisher, the truth and insider information from *Book Proposals That Sell* resonates with my own publishing experiences. Terry Whalin helps would-be authors or experienced writers walk through the critical questions from any acquisitions editor. If you answer these questions, it will help you gain serious consideration for your book idea."

—**Kelly Gallagher**, Vice President, Evangelical Christian Publishers Association

"As an agent, I've read Terry's nonfiction proposals and have always been impressed. He knows how to put together a winning presentation to capture a potential editor's attention and get a decision. In *Book Proposals That Sell*, Terry combines his compassion for writers with his considerable publishing experience to create a must-have book for anyone preparing a nonfiction proposal."

—**Claudia Cross**, Literary Agent, Sterling Lord Literistic, New York City

Many beginning book writers complain that it's harder to write the proposal than the book itself. Until they know how, that's probably true. Terry Whalin knows the secrets of good book proposals. As a writer, he's composed many book proposals; as an editor, he's read hundreds of them. "

—**Cecil Murphey**, writer, co-writer, or ghostwriter of more than 100 books including *Committed But Flawed* and *90 Minutes in Heaven*.

"A well-written book proposal gains attention, piques interest, and provides the information an editor--and later the publicity department--needs to convince not only his editorial staff but the whole publishing team. Terry Whalin provides the know-how to add sales appeal to any book proposal."

—**Les Stobbe**, Literary Agent, Editor-in-Chief, Christian Writer's Guild

"With practical know-how and tons of proven tips, this book is like that wise friend who's been in the business, knows what works and why. Step-by-step, Terry Whalin guides and inspires both beginners and even experienced writers to doing better, successful, meaningful work."

—**Jeanette Thomason**, Acquisition Editor, Revell Books

BOOK PROPOSALS THAT $ELL

21 Secrets to Speed Your Success

W. Terry Whalin

Write Now Publications
Phoenix, Arizona 85013

Book Proposals That Sell
Copyright ©2005 W. Terry Whalin
All rights reserved

Cover and interior design by Walljasper Design
(www.walljasper.com)

Edited by Donna Goodrich and Steve Laube

No part of this book may be reproduced, stored in a retrieval system, or transmitted in any form or by any means–electronic, mechanical, photocopying, recording, or otherwise–without prior permission in writing from the copyright holder except as provided by USA copyright law.

The Thomas Nelson Guide To Writing A Winning Book Proposal by Michael S. Hyatt in Appendix C is used with the permission of the author.

Published by Write Now Publications
A royalty division of ACW Press
5501 N. 7th Ave., #502
Phoenix, Arizona 85013
www.writenowpublications.com

Printed in the United States of America

ISBN 1-932124-64-0

Whalin, Terry.

    Book proposals that sell : 21 secrets to speed your success / by W. Terry Whalin. —
    1st ed. — Phoenix, AZ : Write Now Publications, 2005.

    p. ; cm.
    ISBN: 1-932124-64-0

    1. Book proposals. 2. Authorship—Marketing. 3. Authors and publishers. I. Title.

PN161 .W43 2005
808/.02—dc22

Dedication

To every writer and editor who built so much into my life and
publishing experiences through telling your stories.
Thank you for the joy in the journey.

To every person with dreams and aspirations to get their
ideas into print. May you find in these pages the perfect insight
for your need.

To the One who gives creativity and provides us with
the words when we don't have them.

About the Author

W. TERRY WHALIN KNOWS and understands both sides of the editorial desk—as an editor and a writer. For almost two years, he was the acquisitions editor at Cook Communications Ministries. In that capacity, he located appropriate manuscripts, presented and championed books inside the publishing house, then negotiated and contracted almost 50 different adult and children's books. Terry has also been the fiction acquisitions editor at Howard Publishing Company. He worked as an editor for *Decision* and *In Other Words* magazines and ran a full-time freelance business for seven years. His articles have appeared in more than 50 Christian and general market publications, and he is the author of more than 60 books as well. Terry is the creator of a website for writers of all genres called Right-Writing.com: www.right-writing.com.

A journalism graduate from Indiana University, Terry writes on a wide spectrum of subjects and topics for the magazine and book marketplace—from children to teen to adult. He has co-authored such books as *Running On Ice* by Vonetta Flowers (New Hope Publishers), *Lessons from the Pit, A Successful Veteran of the Chicago Mercantile Exchange Shows Executives How to Thrive in a Competitive Environment* by B. Joseph Leininger (Broadman), *Let the Walls Fall Down* by Bishop Phillip H. Porter, former chairman for Promise Keepers (Creation House) and *First Place* by Carole Lewis (Regal

Books). His latest books include *The Complete Idiot's Guide to Teaching the Bible* (Alpha Books), *Billy Graham* (Bethany House), *Teach Yourself the Bible in 24 Hours* (Alpha Books) and *The Book of Prayers, A Man's Guide to Reaching God* (St. Martin's Press). Two of his numerous biographies are *Sojourner Truth* (Barbour Books) and *Chuck Colson* (Zondervan). In addition, Terry was an instructor for two years for the Institute of Children's Literature, the nation's oldest children's writers' home correspondence course. Also for many years, Terry was an Evangelical Christian Publisher Association Gold Medallion judge in the fiction, inspirational and devotional book categories. He is a member of the American Society of Journalists and Authors, the Evangelical Press Association and the Author's Guild.

Table of Contents

Introduction

Begin at the Beginning

YOU HAVE A BURNING DESIRE to write a nonfiction book. Join the crowd. You might be surprised to learn how many people are writing a book. According to a survey from the Jenkins Group, Inc., a Michigan publishing service firm, 81 percent of Americans feel they should write a book. Jerrold Jenkins, CEO of this group, estimates that more than 6 million Americans have actually written a manuscript—just over 2 percent of the population. *Publisher's Weekly* recently said that more than 1,000 books were published each week during 2003. If you have this desire, how do you begin?

The majority of inexperienced writers will sit down at their computer and pound out their entire manuscript—no matter if it is 40,000 words or 140,000 words. They will begin on the first page and write until the end. It's a major mistake and wasted effort to follow this course of action. On one hand, these writers should be commended because they took the time, energy and discipline to complete their entire book. Many writers begin with good intentions but stop after completing several chapters, deciding that it's too much work. If you fall into the category of a person who has completed a manuscript, you should be congratulated on that large amount of effort and energy.

I've taught at a number of writers' conferences around the U.S. and Canada, and I'm often surprised at the number of people I meet who have invested the time and energy to produce an entire nonfiction manuscript—even some people who "should" know better. During a writers' conference, I arranged a meeting with a leader in a large nonprofit organization (outside of the participants at the conference). We were discussing a possible book project and how we would work together. I explained to him about how the majority of nonfiction books are contracted from a book proposal, not a full-length manuscript. After our hour-long meeting and just before we ended our session, he turned to me and said, "I have a book manuscript that I wrote last year. How do you suggest I get a publisher?" It was as though he didn't listen to the previous conversation. Like many people he had found a subject and a need to address in a book. Not locating a book on this subject, this writer began to doggedly write the entire manuscript from first page to the final page. You have to admire his determination but this type of effort is mostly futile. A book manuscript doesn't contain much of the information or the format for a publisher to make a decision and issue a book contract.

If you are one of those readers who has written a full-length nonfiction manuscript, then don't despair. You need this book more than ever. With your manuscript in hand, you can use the details in this book to create a nonfiction book proposal. This proposal becomes the tool you will need to sell a publisher on your manuscript and convince them that they should publish your book.

Yes, There Is a Difference

Possibly you are an author who writes nonfiction *and* fiction. Because I've worked in both areas of the market—fiction and non-fiction—it's valuable to clarify the distinction. In simple terms, non-fiction is factual whereas fiction is a created story. Sometimes new authors get confused about what they need to market their fiction or nonfiction materials to a publisher.

Two of my published author friends referred someone to me. Often it takes several email exchanges to figure out why I am corresponding with a person and what they need. In this situation, the individual had a proposal for a publisher. If it's a fiction project, then I want to be corresponding with the person using my publisher email address and because of my position with the publisher. On the other hand, if the proposal is a nonfiction project, then I will probably correspond with them through my personal email address. On a rare occasion, I help people get their nonfiction proposals into shape to show a publisher. On other occasions, I will co-author a project with someone and other types of combinations. It takes some exploration to determine what a person needs and if I can help or not.

I began to exchange emails with this unpublished writer who had received a sample book proposal from my published author friends. The writer followed their example and submitted it to a major publishing house which rejected it. This person wondered whether or not he needed my help with the proposal creation. To sort out what needed to be done, I asked the writer to send both proposals to me—the one from the published author friend and the unpublished proposal. I received them within a short period of time.

First I looked at the proposal from my published author friends. I was a bit surprised at the simplicity and lack of completeness of this nonfiction book proposal. As an editor, I've seen many nonfiction book proposals and can quickly evaluate them. Some published authors, after achieving a particular level of book sales and market success, don't have to produce a complete nonfiction book proposal to get a publishing contract. Because of their track record or market for their writings, their submission process is much more simplified than the unpublished author.

Next I looked at the unpublished author's proposal to see if it needed to be reworked before he sent it out to other publishers. At a glance I could see the problem. This author used a nonfiction proposal format for a fiction proposal project. He was wasting his time, energy and postage to market the wrong project in the wrong format. No wonder the publisher rejected his submission.

When I wrote and asked him about it, he quickly responded, "Is the proposal for a fiction proposal different from a nonfiction proposal?"

I told this potential author that the forms were radically different. You are doomed if you follow a nonfiction book proposal format for a fiction submission. I assumed this author was a first time novelist. In general, publishers require these authors to have completed the entire 80,000 to 100,000 word manuscript. It takes a great deal of time and energy to write 100,000 words (typically about a 300 page novel). Usually driven from the need to tell the story, these writers work long hours at their computer to complete the manuscript. For the book to be published, these pages need to be polished, fast-paced and generally excellent. If the novel requires a great deal of work, then it's almost certain to be rejected. Many authors have heard the story of Max Perkins, the editor for Thomas Wolfe. Perkins would pull a little of this and a little of that and from his editorial skills create a classic novel. Those editors are long gone in this business. Instead, the publisher expects the novelist to complete the entire work on speculation—without any certainty of a publishing contract. Why?

I've heard numerous horror stories from long-time editors who contracted a novel because of a dynamic chapter or a terrific plot. Often fiction will change as the story is written. An inexperienced novelist writes their plot into a place where they are stuck and they don't know how to complete the story. This type of situation becomes ugly for both the author and the publisher. From these experiences, publishers have learned to ask for the entire manuscript from first time fiction writers. In addition to the completed manuscript, first time fiction authors need a dynamic synopsis, combined with an outstanding marketing plan, to explain how you are going to personally sell your book. Finally you need to tell the editor a bit about yourself in a short personal bio. Novelists will send out shorter pieces, such as a couple of well-done sample chapters, synopsis, marketing plan and bio, then ask if the editor wants to see the entire manuscript. An excellent book on this process for fiction authors is *Your Novel Proposal From Creation to Contract* by Blythe Camenson and Marshall J. Cook (http://snipurl.com/novel). [See appendix F for an explanation of the snipurl web address tool used throughout the book.]

The story for nonfiction is totally different. This book focuses on nonfiction and how you can write a nonfiction book proposal and get a publishing contract. Several years ago, literary agent Jennifer Rudolph-Walsh was interviewed in a writers' newsletter. Over ten years earlier Rudolph-Walsh was an agent with the Virginia Barber Literary Agency and pulled in a $400,000 advance for Ethan Hawke's first novel. She said, "A well thought out proposal with an outline and a table of contents and maybe one to three sample chapters is enough. A friend of mine had a whole nonfiction manuscript and couldn't sell it." Rudolph-Walsh had the author chop off the first three chapters, then she sent it out and got $550,000 for something that couldn't be sold for any price only four months earlier.

What counts in a nonfiction proposal is the promise of what's to come with the finished manuscript and the editor's potential to push the manuscript slightly in one direction or another. My experience says that the editor doesn't push it much in the process, but because a proposal is in more of an "outline" format, it has the illusion of the editor pushing it. Normally I've written each of my nonfiction books exactly like I wrote them in the proposal—chapter by chapter.

Keep these statistics in mind as you think about your nonfiction book proposal. At any given time, 500,000 proposals and manuscripts circulate across the United States. With good writing skills and using the secrets in this book, you can beat these odds and get a contract. One major publisher received over 6,000 unsolicited manuscripts and proposals in a year, yet didn't accept a single one. These thousands of proposals weren't written well and didn't include the necessary elements of a proposal, nor were they appropriate for this particular publisher. The writer has to fulfill every expectation in order to stand out from the other submissions.

You should be congratulated for your purchase of this book because you have saved yourself hours of effort and potential heartache. As you write, keep in mind this important statistic: *nine out of ten nonfiction books are sold from a nonfiction book proposal.*

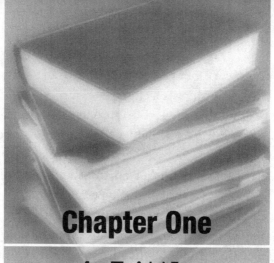

Chapter One

A Little Background Story

AT A SMALL COFFEE SHOP I MET Joe Leininger who had traded for ten years in the Eurodollar Pit of the Chicago Mercantile. In that incredible greed-centered environment, Joe thrived and made a million dollars every year for ten years and then retired. He had some strange and fascinating stories about his experiences on the Merc floor, which he began pounding out in a nonfiction book manuscript. While the writing experience was cathartic for Joe and lots of fun, he wanted a regular publisher to produce his book manuscript. Unlike the average author, Joe had a few personal connections with some publishers. He thought this would give his manuscript an advantage for publication so he submitted it for their consideration. After several weeks, each package returned with a rejection note. Without professional guidance, Joe was unsure how to get his book published and into the traditional bookstores. Because of his personal resources, he could self-publish his book and have a garage full of his work, but he was wise enough to understand that, in general, book publishing is a closed system. For your book to be sold in the bookstore, it needs to go through a traditional publisher who has a distribution channel for these stores. To test this, pick any self-publisher, go into your local retail bookstore and search for any title from this publisher on the shelf. You will be hard pressed to find much (if any) of this type of product.

I met with Joe and he gave me a copy of his manuscript. From my reading, I could see potential but I also spotted a key flaw. Joe included fascinating stories about his experiences in the pit but these stories had no takeaway information for the reader. He missed passing along the lessons from his experiences to other people—whether they ever saw the crazed action on the floor of the Chicago Mercantile or not. Readers approach books from a selfish viewpoint. Every book has to answer the key question, "What's in this book *for me?*"

With some prodding on my part, Joe produced a series of 16 lessons about life and success from his work in the Pit. These lessons became the backbone of the book proposal that I wrote. Eventually Broadman and Holman published our book entitled *Lessons from the Pit*. Each lesson became a single chapter in the book.

Every reader approaches nonfiction books with the desire to learn something for himself and take away some information or insight from their reading. The material has to be told in an engaging manner, but every sentence must be written with the reader in mind. The same approach is necessary when writing a book proposal. You are writing the proposal to attract an agent or editor, and eventually the publisher. If you focus the entire book manuscript on what you want to say without thinking of the reader, it will not be a book a publisher will want to print.

Always remember one basic lesson about nonfiction book publishing: In general, publishers buy book *proposals* for nonfiction—not book *manuscripts*. I know Joe has multiple ideas and hopes to write other books. The last time I checked, he was pounding out another complete manuscript. I trust he learned this basic lesson. Certain people are doomed through their stubborn persistence to repeat the lessons from the past. If you follow the advice in this book, however, you can benefit from my long-term experience in the publishing world.

Chapter Two

Why Publishers Prefer Nonfiction Proposals

IN THE CASE OF NONFICTION, EDITORS, agents and publishing executives prefer to read a nonfiction proposal instead of a full-length manuscript. For several years, I've been an acquisitions editor or the first person to read the nonfiction proposal or manuscript that comes into the publishing house. I've interfaced with the publisher's existing authors and talked with them about new projects. I've also championed many first time authors' proposals inside the publishing house, presented them to the publication board (the decision-making body in most houses), worked up the financial figures (an internal document which no one sees outside the publishing house), then negotiated with the author or their agent on the final contract. I have firsthand, insider knowledge about the consideration process and can give you a glimpse at how your proposal will be processed and handled.

As you think about approaching a traditional publisher, keep the following points in mind:

1) *If the publisher has been in business for some time, a key and regular part of their acquisitions strategy is to return to their existing authors (provided these books are selling well) and ask these authors for additional projects.*

If a publisher has a book with an author who has been consistently selling in the market, they have less risk to publish another book from this same author and sell it to the audience. Like many other businesses, publishing is about managing risk. To take a completed 60,000 word manuscript and produce it into a book will cost the publisher anywhere between $25,000 and $50,000. This number isn't a typographical error. Recently I attended the annual conference of the American Society of Journalists and Authors in New York City. One of the participants on a panel about book proposals was Brian DiForio, a New York literary agent who is a former editorial director for some major publishers. He presented to the conference some even higher production numbers, saying, "Even with a modest advance of $20,000 to $30,000, the overall costs for the publisher are between $75,000 and $100,000. You are proposing a business decision like any proposal to a bank." These numbers do not include marketing or advertising expenses nor do they account for a large advance for the author (which increases the risk for the publisher). The number is pure production costs, editorial expenses and design costs for the cover and interior pages of the book.

Publishers make this type of financial investment in an author with care, forethought and wisdom—especially if they want to stay in the book business for many years. If you are writing nonfiction children's books, the above figure *doubles*. When I mention this information at a writers' conference, I can hear the visible gasps in the room. Many parents have read stacks of 24- or 32-page full-color books to their children. They've seen the few words on the page and probably believed they could have easily written a better book. They don't realize, however, that the production numbers for these books can vary from $150,000 to $200,000. The reason for these costs is because when it comes to children's books, the publisher normally purchases full rights from the artist to whoever owns the artwork in these books. In general, these artists/illustrators do not receive a royalty for their work, only a flat fee, and that price adds to the production expense.

Before I began working inside a book publishing house, I had written more than 50 nonfiction books, ranging from children's to adult books. I have never self-published a book and always worked through traditional publishers. However, I was unaware of the financial production numbers for nonfiction books and I found it shocking—and something critical for potential authors to understand. The author never sees these figures for their books as the publisher doesn't reveal them throughout the contract negotiation process. A publisher will produce these financial calculations as simply a part of good business practices. As an author, understanding this helped me see publishing as a business. Authors have huge amounts of time and emotional investment in their words. When I saw these production numbers, I understood that the publisher, not the author, has the largest out-of-pocket cash investment in a book.

Inside the publisher, the editor will gather a sales projection about how many copies the sales department believes they can sell of your title the first year. That sales figure will be used to calculate the production costs of ink, paper and binding for various amounts of printing (5,000, 10,000 or 15,000 copies). As the initial print number is raised, the cost per book decreases. You may ask, So why not print a large volume each time? The answer is, if the publisher prints a large number of copies, then he has to store those copies in their warehouse (read cost and expense), plus make sure they actually sell those copies within a year's timeframe. The cost of tying up financial resources in storing and warehousing books that aren't selling is large. Also the federal government taxes publishers on each copy in storage. These tax rules have forced publishers to think long and hard about how many copies of each book to print.

Inside my former publisher, we calculated the overall printing details of the book (paperback with general publishing look or hardcover with jacket) and the number of books to print before offering a book contract. In short, publishers pour a great deal of work into their books and financial projections before they call you and offer a nonfiction book contract. Understanding this process helps you see some of the reasons it takes such a long time for an author to receive a publishing contract.

I know this section took a brief aside to explain about the inner workings inside a publishing house. Now let's return to my original point about book acquisition. Often the publisher returns to an author with whom they have already published a book. If the publisher takes a second or third book from the same author, they are investing in that author's career and trying to build that author's audience and market. If the author's books are selling well, then the publisher will be eager for another project. Each week, publishers monitor sales numbers on their books to see if particular authors merit another book contract.

Many writers focus only on the creative aspects of writing a book and getting it published, but the executives inside a publishing house are business people who want to sell books and turn a profit at the end of the day. It's a delicate balance between creating the best possible product and assuring that each product has the best opportunity to sell into the market and reach the target audience.

2) *Editors and agents do a great deal more than read unsolicited manuscripts.*

As an acquisitions editor, I didn't passively sit and wait for these projects to land in my in-basket. Rather, I made it a daily goal to be proactive in looking for the right manuscripts. Because I've been involved in publishing for many years, I have a series phone number and other contact information for these bestselling authors and their agents in my address book. Actively I telephoned and emailed these authors to see what they were working on and to discover if anything new might be appropriate for my publishing house. While these authors might not have published with my publisher, each one had a successful sales track record. I understood my publishing house might have to pay higher advances and royalties for these projects than they would have to pay for a first-time author. At the same time, I understood these published authors already had a reader following; thus, this involved less business risk and gave us a greater chance for success.

It's not easy to acquire these published authors because their schedule is often filled for several years. In my conversations or emails, I would try and suggest possible projects for them to consider. Sometimes during the conversation I would see a spark of interest. On one occasion, I was talking in detail with a bestselling fiction author but I was talking with her about a nonfiction book project. In the early days of her career, she wrote nonfiction but now her writing schedule was filled with fiction and storytelling. "I know a nonfiction book would allow different kinds of media possibilities than my fiction," she said. I could hear the passion in her voice about the topic we were discussing for this nonfiction book. I also knew this author's agent was discouraging her from talking with me or placing a project with my publishing house. I understand that authors will listen to the perspective of their agent but ultimately they are in charge of their writing schedule. This story gives you a glimpse into the type of proactive acquisitions activity an editor can take.

Another tactic I took when I talked with published authors was to see if their files contained an unsold book proposal. Often there is a good reason why this proposal is unsold. Maybe it needs reshaping for the marketplace or audience, yet from a published author, it's worth the time and consideration from an editor. I also looked for out-of-print books which could be repackaged with a new title and updated information to bring this author to my publishing house. Sometimes an author has a book project for which they have considerable passion but it quickly faded out of print with another publisher. A book goes out of print for many reasons, some of which have nothing to do with the content of the book. Maybe the book had a terrible cover or a weak title. Possibly because of personnel changes within a publishing house, the book sold poorly and was taken out of print in a short amount of time (less than two years).

It was rare for our publishing house to take these out of prints but in certain cases, these books were contracted. If I could create a new package, new title, different content or possibly a different emphasis *and* it was a better fit for our publishing house than the previous publisher, we then contracted the book for publication. With one of these books I acquired, I know the publisher is going to get endorsements from high profile authors, including an eye-catching foreword, because they repackaged an out-of-print book. I used a variety of different strategies in the acquisition of books rather than taking books from new and unpublished authors.

As a reader who wants to get your nonfiction book published, why do you care? As you increase your understanding about the ways publishers operate and make decisions, you will be able to shape your nonfiction book proposal in a way that will meet their expectations and needs. Never forget that *knowledge is power.*

Through proactive prodding of best-selling authors, I would often find a book valuable for my publisher to consider. When I spent this type of personal energy grooming established authors, I was not reading or actively looking at manuscripts from unknown authors. What this means to you is that an editor is not spending all their time working on manuscripts from unknown authors.

It is challenging for unpublished authors to receive constructive feedback from an editor. Because of the volume of material coming across my desk, occasionally I would see a nonfiction proposal which had a nugget of potential. But maybe the nugget was buried on page 5 of the proposal, plus it lacked a number of essential elements to build a complete proposal. If the project was about 80 to 90 percent of what I needed, then I would correspond with the author and get what I needed to build that final 20 or 10 percent. And what if I read an unsolicited nonfiction book proposal which contains only the nugget and needs a greater percentage of work? Unfortunately this proposal is returned with a standard rejection letter. Because of the sheer volume of proposals, I'm unable to add a personal note of encouragement. There aren't enough hours available for this type of detailed critique work on unpublished proposals. I'm honestly trying to help you understand the editor and the type of pressures in every day editorial work.

Please don't despair about the shape of your idea, manuscript or nonfiction book proposal. In the pages that follow, I'm going to give you a series of tips to catch the editor (or agent's) attention. It's important that you understand where the editor is coming from—to lessen your own frustration at their slow response or lack of response.

Besides continual networking with established authors for projects, acquisitions editors have other events crowding their daily schedule. These events don't happen on a single day but often editors are in meetings—lots of meetings—which may include:
- title meetings (to discuss and select the title for a contracted book—and these meetings can take many hours)
- editorial planning meetings (weekly and several hour events at my publisher discussing procedures and other mundane but necessary things)
- concept meetings (where the title has been selected and you need to talk about the contents with your colleagues in the marketing and design areas—for example, what the cover could be for a particular book)

- cover design meetings (several of these meetings where the editors, designers and marketing people look at first covers, then another meeting to look at the covers as they are closer to being in final shape)
- editorial meetings (meetings with fellow editors to determine which projects move to the publishing leadership)
- publication board (the leadership of the publisher who determine which books are contracted and published)
- marketing meetings and
- sales meetings.

No matter what job title an editor has within a publishing house, they handle a plethora of duties and are often overworked and short on time.

Beyond the regularly scheduled group meetings, individual meetings about major and minor aspects of publishing are common. If a current author calls or emails about something, sometimes the only way to answer the request is to hold another meeting. My responsibility was to serve the publishing house and serve my authors (any author with a published book with my publisher). The acquisitions editor is often the public face of the publishing house. If an agent or an author calls with a problem, I actively worked on connecting with the people to solve this situation. Each one of these incidents takes time away from reading proposals and processing unpublished authors.

Another common event inside publishing houses that can stir many meetings is an acquisition of another publisher or another line of books from a publisher. If you read *Publisher's Weekly* (which I highly recommend so you can be aware of publishing changes), you will begin to understand that occasionally publishers will purchase entire lines of books from another publisher.

At my former publisher, this type of acquisition added 350 titles to our backlist. For a minute, imagine that you were one of those authors whose book was suddenly sold to a new publisher. Under normal circumstances, when a publisher is sold, the editors and leaders of a publishing house will cease their communication with most authors and literary agents as they try to quietly transfer the entire product line. The new publishing house that buys the older material is suddenly deluged with phone calls from these authors and/or their agents who want to introduce themselves, find out about their books and have answered a multitude of other questions.

When a publishing house acquires a huge backlist of books or another publisher, this acquisition pushes out every other decision within the publishing house (including whether or not to publish new books). For a matter of months during the transition, this decision is all consuming and few new books with unknown authors are contracted. You should know about this factor and take it into consideration as you send out your nonfiction book proposal. If a publisher has recently acquired another publisher, it might not be the best time to submit your proposal.

Editors also occasionally attend conferences—sometimes to improve their own skills as an editor and other times to teach workshops and meet face-to-face with potential authors. These sessions often require five to seven days on the road and away from their desk. When I returned from such a trip, I had phone calls to return and urgent editorial matters to handle. The unsolicited manuscripts get pushed into a pile to be processed later.

Why have I told you these details about an editor's task? Because my goal is to help you understand that the publisher, editor or agent isn't sitting around with an empty agenda waiting for your book proposal. Many authors complain about the length of time for a decision or any type of response, but there are many good reasons for such delays. The editors inside a publishing house are focused on current work which will hopefully lead to profitability for the publisher. Your proposal or idea may have potential earnings but the editors are much more focused on the accepted manuscripts already in front of them.

I commonly tell authors if they want my instant response, I can give it—but it will not be what they want to hear. If an author or an agent pushes for a decision, the instant and easiest answer for an editor to give is "no, thank you." As an editor, when you turn down a project, you risk possibly missing a bestseller such as a *Prayer of Jabez* or a *Purpose Driven Life* type of book. From my years of publishing experience, I know these particular books came into their respective publisher not as an *unsolicited manuscript*. These two bestselling books didn't come in over the transom or unsolicited. They came to the publisher through some of the other means that editors acquire books.

It's relatively quick to decide to say no, stuff a form rejection into the envelope or paste it into a return email. I realize that "yes" is the only answer an author wants to hear about their work; however, a publisher's phone call or email that a publishing contract is on the way to an author often requires volumes of time.

One Thursday in the publishing house, I answered my telephone. (I always attempted to do this myself, rather than letting it go to my voice mail.) On the phone was an unpublished author. (By the way, as a professional writer, I almost never cold call a publishing house. It's one of the best ways to make a lasting and often negative impression.)

This author began, "Mark _____ (a specific name) over at _____ (another publisher) recommended that I give you a call." I warmly responded to this opening because I've known Mark for many years and see him at various conferences and conventions. Then she launched into her pitch about how she had written a children's book to teach the young child about the danger of AIDS. Because we published children's books *and* we accepted unsolicited manuscripts from anyone, I encouraged her to submit the manuscript.

She paused and said, "I live in Texas but I'm in town at the moment. Can I drop it by your front desk?" I responded, affirming that would be fine. It would have been a refusal if she had tried to meet with me (something else you normally don't want to do). Then she continued, "I'm only in town until Monday. Do you think I could get a decision by then?"

The question revealed her complete ignorance of book publishing. From my perspective, publishing is a consensus-building process. To get a book contract, the acquisitions editor may be the first person to convince. Then the acquisitions editor has to convince many other people within the company about the salability of a particular manuscript. Normally the various book editors meet together and process the best submissions. During this session, the editors make suggestions for improvement and the team selects only the best material to go ahead into the process to the publication board. The "pub" board generally meets once or twice a month. They can call a special meeting but it's rare. This board includes the leadership of the publishing house (president, vice-president of product or editorial, vice-president of marketing, vice-president of sales, etc.) and is made up of five to twenty people. Some publishers include their key sales personnel in this process because these salespeople are the ones to actually convince a customer to purchase the book. The acquisitions editor prepares the presentation material on each book which includes the nonfiction book proposal. Several weeks ahead of the pub board meeting, this material is distributed to each member of the committee. Sometimes, because of the member's schedule, they don't read the material ahead of time. Other times they have read through the presentations and prepared questions for the acquisitions editor.

During the meeting, the acquisitions editor presents your book to the committee, fields their questions and defends the necessity of publishing this book, then the members vote whether a title is appropriate for them to publish or not. At many publishers, prior to the meeting, specific finances for the book have been prepared.

After a "yes" decision, the author or agent is contacted and the acquisitions editor negotiates the specifics of the publishing contract.

While the acquisitions editor may be the initial person to convince, he has to persuade many other people that your nonfiction book proposal will be a great "fit" for the publishing house. It is not a snap decision.

Now let's return to the woman who wanted to drop off her children's book on AIDS at my office, then get a decision with a three-day turnaround. This author followed through with her promise and I received a call from the front desk that the package was waiting. Later that afternoon, I opened the package, curious about the contents. In this case, the woman had very primitive looking illustrations combined with unusual words—especially for children, using explicit vocabulary about the different ways AIDS can be transmitted. I reacted negatively because the manuscript used words that I would never promote or publish in children's material. In a glance, I knew I would be returning this manuscript. Then I took a second look inside the package. Where was the mechanism to return the materials? This author didn't include a self-addressed stamped envelope for returning her manuscript (SASE) nor an email address (another cost effective means of communication).

Like many other publishers, our company had a policy of not returning any unsolicited manuscript without an SASE. Just imagine this unplanned and unbudgeted postage expense for a publisher who receives literally thousands of unsolicited manuscripts. This is simply a wise business decision. I tossed the children's book manuscript onto a pile. Knowing authors, I figured she would be calling me about it before too much time passed. Sure enough, a few weeks later the children's author from Texas phoned and asked about her AIDS children's book. I instantly recalled the situation and explained that her manuscript wasn't appropriate for our publisher. I also explained our company policy about not returning manuscripts without postage and asked if she wanted the manuscript.

"Oh, I want it back," she exclaimed. She sent the return postage came and I returned the manuscript. The final blow was that she called again and asked, "Since my children's book wasn't right for you, could you recommend somewhere else I can send it?"

From my extensive contacts within the publishing community, I could have easily recommended an editor at a different publishing house. But I flashed back to my introduction to this author, "Mark _____ at _____ recommended that I call you." I knew better than to recommend another editor because soon she would be using my name in the next call. "Terry Whalin recommended that I call you...."

Instead I told her that no one specific came to mind for her project. Instead I recommended that she go to her local library and use the latest *Writer's Market*. The moral is: Watch yourself when you interact with editors at publishing houses; we have long memories. You only have one chance to make a first impression. I'm certain this author believed she was making an impression with her personal phone calls and deliberate interaction. In publishing, it's going to be the writing and the fit with the idea which will ultimately make the difference.

3. Editors are reading submissions from agents and other people with whom they have a personal relationship.

Because editors receive such a high volume of inappropriate material from the general public, many publishers have tried to limit unsolicited manuscripts and proposals. Some have even closed the door for these submissions, returning the manuscripts unopened.

These editors do read manuscripts from authors they meet at writers' conference, but when working in their offices, they only read book proposals or manuscripts from literary agents. In fact, most editors prefer to read a proposal from an agent because a good agent is familiar with the range and subject of books from the publishing house. In many cases, agents have become a sifting method for the editor.

As an editor, I am constantly interacting with various agents and their authors. Literary agents represent some (not all) of our authors. I'm constantly learning and gathering information about different agents and this information helps me acquire excellent books. For example, I'll ask an author, "Tell me a bit of the history with this particular proposal. How has it evolved? What role (if any) did your agent have in this process?" After asking these leading types of questions, I listen carefully for the response. I'm not gathering the information to tell anyone, but simply for my own insight into a particular agent.

I've contracted several books with different authors from one literary agent in particular. Often without prodding, these authors have told me how their proposal was kicked back repeatedly from this agent with notes for revision. Before becoming a literary agent, this woman spent many years working with different authors and inside different publishing houses. From this long-time career, she is now guiding different authors on the specifics of their manuscripts and proposals. As an editor, it's comforting to receive a well-crafted submission from this agent. When you ask her questions about the proposal, she answers with confidence because she's worked intimately with the author on crafting the details.

Not every author needs this type of back-and-forth editorial crafting for a proposal. Some will be able to create their own well-done proposal without guidance from a literary agent. Each situation is different. Hopefully from this single example, however, you can see the difference an agent can make in the submission process. Over years of working together, when I receive proposals from certain agents, I tend to read them quicker and bring them into the consideration process quicker.

Each time an agent sends a proposal for one of their clients, they are also projecting their own professionalism and knowledge about the marketplace. As an editor, I recognized the range of attention to the submission process even from literary agents. Some submit well-crafted proposals from their authors; others do not. The editor quickly learns which agents have good material and which agents they can ignore or delay the reading of their authors' proposals.

When an editor travels to writers' conferences, they are looking for book proposals from people they know or whose names they recognize. They will actively seek these proposals and find the time to read them earlier than the unsolicited book proposals.

After reading these paragraphs about an agent, do not despair because you haven't found one. In the pages ahead, I'm going to tell you step-by-step how to create an excellent book proposal which will catch an editor's (or agent's) attention.

4) *The unsolicited manuscripts and proposals are often the last material that an editor reads on their desk.*

Okay. Here's the straight scoop on the editor: You can see from the previous sections that the editor is often away from his or her desk and can barely process the urgent material that comes into the mailbox. If the editor travels often, he or she falls even further behind on processing mail and manuscripts. As an acquisitions editor, I traveled about a week a month and during some times of the year, this amount increased to almost two weeks a month. In the middle of my other responsibilities, *I would often go two or three or four weeks without opening a single new proposal or manuscript.* I piled them high on my desk and sometimes on a nearby bookshelf.

Once when I explained my particular system for unsolicited manuscripts to an editor at another publishing house, he said, "My assistant opens my mail and processes some of it for me." (Translated, this means that this assistant read the mail, then rejects some of it.) I smiled into the phone and said, "I sure would like to find that assistant in my office."

At my publisher, our group of editors had an editorial assistant but she was mostly working at other tasks and could barely sort the department mail—much less help individual editors sort through unsolicited manuscripts. If you addressed the proposal with my name on it, then it came to my desk and I would be the one to open and process it.

I've gone into detail about the various tasks of an editor in the publishing house—and I haven't even mentioned editing books (another part of the normal job). My purpose thus far has been to increase your understanding of the pressure and stress of an editor so you will see even more clearly the importance of putting together an acceptable and enticing book proposal.

5) *Every editor and agent is looking for new writing talent and proposals that will fit their particular publishing needs.*

Don't be discouraged about the daunting task of reaching an editor with your precious book idea. As someone who has written and published with a variety of publishers and magazines, I understand rejection. The publishing business requires thick skin and confidence in your abilities. I've been rejected many times—more than I can count, yet I continue to send out book proposals and try new publishers. Rejection is hard for many people, but when it happens to you, you should remember that editors are not rejecting you as a person. A manuscript is rejected for many reasons. You have to persist and continue to market your materials and search for the right fit in a publishing house.

Many writers grow discouraged and quit sending in their work after one or two rejections. If you prepare an excellent nonfiction proposal, then continue to look for the right publisher. If you've done the necessary work to prepare a full-length book proposal (and many have not completed this work), you can have confidence as you send it out. Publishers and agents need new ideas and new proposals because this is the lifeblood of the business. Publishing may look like an exclusive club with little opportunity for new people. It's not. Every publisher is looking for new talent and they need and want your book proposals. The key is to give the publisher details and information needed in a book proposal.

If you don't understand the book proposal system, your proposals may be inappropriate, incomplete or underdeveloped. After weeks or months of waiting for a response, you may find only a form rejection letter.

In the pages that follow, you are going to learn why you bought this book. The investment is going to pay off for you—but only if you follow *every* detail and *every* secret. Each of these secrets is critical to your success in marketing your nonfiction book proposal to the publishing world.

I'll be the first to admit that writing a book proposal involves considerable effort. It's not a simple document. Most of them range from 15 to 30 pages and contain a great deal of information. This proposal is critical to your success in the nonfiction book area, so don't shy away from the effort required to properly construct it.

Chapter Three

How Do You Follow the Trends in Publishing?

FROM THE MINUTE THIS WRITER shook my hand and sat down at a small table, she looked nervous. Both of us were attending a writers' conference and now we were meeting for a 15-minute appointment. A key benefit of these conferences is this opportunity for the writer to talk one-on-one with an editor representing a publishing house. Personally I enjoy these events and see them as a time to meet people, encourage them and possibly find a new author.

She reached for a strand of her blonde, shoulder-length hair and nervously twisted it as she talked about her writing. Reaching into her satchel, she pulled out her proposal and gingerly slid it across the table into my hands. I thanked her for the chance to read it and took a few minutes to flip through the pages and study it. She watched me carefully and her breathing seemed shallow like she was unconsciously holding her breath. For the first time, an editor was holding her work.

As a writer, I've been in the same position as this author so I empathized with her anxiety and vulnerable feelings. You are giving a part of yourself into my hands as an editor. After possibly weeks or days of attempting to select the perfect word, you are letting this material fly into the market and to someone who could potentially offer you a book contract. It's a trust I don't take lightly. Part of your risk as an author is putting your work out into the marketplace. If the material remains in a file folder or in your computer, it will never reach the audience. No one likes to be rejected or told their work needs improvement or changes. No one likes hearing that their work isn't appropriate for a particular publishing house. Rejection of your work, however, is a part of the writer's life. Remember again that it's not *you* personally that is being rejected. It's your manuscript and its appropriateness for a particular house. We can't say it often enough that publishing is a business. Editors are not gods and we do make mistakes, but at the same time we are paid for our years of experience and our track record of making good decisions.

Years ago, I interviewed bestselling author Charles R. Swindoll, known to most people as Chuck. We talked about this issue of elevating people and holding them in esteem. It's good to respect people but as Chuck told me, "Even the President of the United States puts his pants on one leg at a time." Then this Texas-born author told me something I've never forgotten, "We're all like a bunch of guys in the back of a pick-up truck, trying to get our stuff together."

In the last chapter, I mentioned the large financial commitment a publisher makes to produce your nonfiction book. These decisions are made carefully and with the expectation that the book will earn a profit and achieve a relative measure of success. This measure of success is different for each book. Sometimes success is 5,000 copies in the first year of publication and other times it is measured as 100,000 copies in the first year of publication. Different publishing variables determine these numbers.

In this chapter, you'll receive some basic insight into books and industry-related statistics, including a series of resources so you can learn more about publishing and the ever-changing state of the book marketplace. Finally, in a big-picture sense, we'll examine a series of publishing trends. Why do you care about such information? Because the more you know about how publishing works, the better chance you'll have of landing a nonfiction book contract. Also, from this information you will be more knowledgeable to send your nonfiction book proposal to an appropriate agent or editor.

Picking a Bestseller

People usually take out their pens and paper at a writers' conference when I talk about this topic of picking a bestseller. Everyone wants to know the secret. According to an article by Ed Christman in *The Book Standard* on January 27, 2005,

> The top 200 bestselling books of 2004 moved a combined 73.5 million copies, or 10.8% of the total 677.9 million units sold, during the year, as measured by Neilsen BookScan. Among those 200 titles were 10 that exceeded a million copies each, 22 that moved between a million and 500,000 units and 101 that sold between half a million and 200,000 copies.

It's very rare in the book-selling business to be in this top percentage. Few publishers can find these types of books or this level of success for their authors. At a writer's conference, during an editor's supper, I was discussing best-selling books with the editorial director of a large publishing house. In one of the magazines that crossed my desk, I read about a large New York celebration HarperCollins threw in honor of Rick Warren and his achievement of crossing the 20 million copy milestone for sales of *The Purpose Driven Life* (Zondervan Publishing House). Billionaire Rupert Murdoch, who owns HarperCollins, attended this celebration. He said in this article, "When one of our authors sells a million books, we think he's a genius. When a book sells 20 million copies, we think we're geniuses." It's a funny quotation and everyone at the table laughed—except this editorial director with years in the publishing business.

"That is the most ridiculous bunch of nonsense," he exclaimed, then he continued, "I talked with the editors at Zondervan and they told me that they only projected to sell 300,000 copies of *The Purpose Driven Life*. Everything over that is simply God's work and unexplainable in human terms."

The wisdom of this conversation made sense to me. Everyone in publishing has high hopes and expectations when a book is published. Editorial, marketing and sales do their best effort with the amount of work and time on their hands, but the sales results for a particular book are often out of our control.

Michael Korda, long-time editor-in-chief of Simon and Schuster, wrote *Making the List, A Cultural History of the American Bestseller 1900-1999 as seen through the annual bestseller lists of Publishers Weekly* (Barnes & Noble Books, 2001). With a little commentary about a particular ten-year segment, Korda walks readers through the best-selling books of the last century. Because I love books and I'm interested in what gets on these lists, I devoured this particular book. In his introduction, Korda writes,

> The bestseller list, in fact, presents us with a kind of corrective reality. It tells us what we're actually reading (or, at least, what we're actually buying) as opposed to what we thing we ought to be reading, or would like other people to believe we're buying. Like stepping on the scales, it tells us the truth, however unflattering, and is therefore, taken over the long haul, a pretty good way of assess-

ing our culture and of judging how, if any we have changed.

From studying these lists, I learned that the bestsellers have little predictability or explanation. In the 1950s, the card game called canasta swept the nation and many people marched into their local booksellers and purchased a how-to-play-canasta book. Two of these books made the bestseller lists for this era. Here's one of the nuggets of truth Korda unearths from his research: "The lesson is, yes, there *are* rules, but they don't apply to writers of real talent, and they're not absolute for anybody. The only thing you can say for sure is that, yes, the ability to tell a story matters a lot, in fiction and in nonfiction, and having something new and interesting to say about familiar subjects is maybe at the heart of it all."

In the final pages of this book, Korda summarizes his conclusions saying, "As for nonfiction, how different is the list today from what Americans were reading a hundred years ago? Not very, is the answer. Celebrities, political history and scandal, self-help and cookbooks brought Americans in to the bookstore, as now, and what seems most new is usually just a gloss on the old."

I recommend studying *Making the List* as it is a good tool to learn about the publishing business. This book also affirms the certainty of uncertainty. It's unpredictable which books will become bestsellers and which books, after a time in the market, will be sent to the bargain book table for a quick sale. *Making the List* is a solid lesson for anyone who wants to write nonfiction books.

Several Resources to Follow the Publishing Marketplace

The world of publishing is constantly changing. One company acquires books from another company. An editor moves from magazine editing into book editing. A book editor decides to take the leap and become a literary agent. There is no definitive way to keep tabs on the ever-shifting marketplace but the following resources can help.

One of the best resources for the general market is *Publisher's Weekly* at http://snipurl.com/pweek. Subscribers have access to an online version of this magazine and also receive regular emails. If the cost of the magazine is prohibitive, read it at your local library. Almost every public library in the U.S. takes this publication to keep up on the current and forthcoming books. For many years, I read this publication every week at the library. *Publisher's Weekly* gives you a great education in publishing.

Another resource is *Publisher's Lunch*. A subscriber version is available for a nominal fee or you can get the free email listing which contains a great deal of information about publishing. You can learn more at http://snipurl.com/publunch.

If you are looking for book publishing statistics, a general website of information that is updated on an ongoing basis is http://snipurl.com/bkstat. By taking the time to study these publishing statistics, you will increase your understanding of this world and your nonfiction book proposals will be stronger as a result.

There are many different resources but I want to give you several key attitudes which are just as important.

1. Make a consistent commitment to stay current and learn about the market so you won't look totally out of date. It has been several years since I left my position as acquisitions editor at Cook Communications. In the final days of my work there, I continued to receive submissions addressed to the previous editor, Jan Dennis (now a literary agent). Jan had left the company at least three years earlier, yet some writers continued sending manuscripts addressed to him. Obviously these writers were using ancient marketing information. It made an instant impression on the editor, but not a positive one. Always make sure you have the current editor and that you spell their name right. Details are important.

2. Beyond the commitment, you need to make time in your schedule to do something rare these days—read. I see the surveys

about literacy in the U.S. and less people are reading—anything—books, magazines, newspapers, etc. You have to make a regular effort to read a variety of genres. I take about 50 different magazines (no exaggeration here). Do I read every article on every page? No, but I take the time to absorb a great deal of information from each magazine. Which magazines are publishing what types of articles? Who is the editor at what magazine and is anything changing? Change can be an opportunity for you as a writer to form a relationship with a new editor. Watch for those opportunities in the marketplace because they can open new doors for your writing.

3. Understand that you will not always get it right. The publishing world continues to constantly evolve and change and it's hard for anyone to keep up with all of the bits of information. Balance being vigilant and continuing to learn about the market with giving yourself a break if you address the wrong editor or spell an editor's name wrong or send your manuscript to the wrong place. Learn from your mistakes and it will make you a better writer in the days ahead.

Six Publishing Trends for Your Awareness

The world of publishing is constantly changing. The various trends in this section, along with my comments, are culled from my years of working within the industry. My aim is that you begin to see some of these emerging patterns and tap into the evolving market as you write your nonfiction book proposals. To successfully market your nonfiction books, you will need to monitor these trends and see where your ideas and proposals fit into the publishing culture.

Trend #1: Books Fit into a Multimedia World

Reading continues to decline and each year statistics show less people buying books and reading. Our attention span is less and the tendency to surf the Internet and different websites only lessens this attention span. According to the May 23, 2003 issue of *Publisher's Weekly*, "people reduced their time reading between 1996 and 2001 to 2.1 hours/month." (http://snipurl.com/bkstat)

Trend #2: The Distinction Between Religious Publishers and General Market Publishers Continues To Blur.

Several years ago I attended a Book Expo in Los Angeles. During the previous year, HarperCollins Publishers had purchased Zondervan Publishing House. The books from HarperCollins are distinct from Zondervan. I was fascinated to see a general market Clive Barker horror fiction beside the New International Version of the Bible from Zondervan. It was only a taste of what continues in the publishing market.

At the time of this writing, Simon and Schuster announced the launch of a children's line of inspirational books. TimeWarner has a strong line of faith books through WarnerFaith and now CenterStreet. A recent issue of *Publisher's Weekly* promoted a new Tim LaHaye book (of *Left Behind*/Tyndale fame) with the general market publisher Kensington Books. I believe we can expect to see these distinctions continue to blur in the days ahead.

Trend #3: The Continual Proliferation of Products

Each year the number of books published continues to increase. In the April 24, 2004 issue of *The Wall Street Journal*, R.R. Bowker reported 2.8 million books in print in 2004. http://snipurl.com/bkstat. The increasing number of products causes an overall problem with less people reading and purchasing books. How can your particular book catch the attention of its designed audience? It's a trend to watch.

Trend #4: Multiplication in the Channels for Books

Remember when you had to go to a bookstore to purchase books? According to Jerrold Jenkins at the Jenkins Group, 70 percent of U.S. adults have not been in a bookstore in the last five years. (http://snipurl.com/bkstat) Increasingly books are purchased in other places such as online, in Target or Wal-Mart or Price Clubs or chain stores like Borders or Barnes & Noble. Increasingly books are sold directly to the consumers and also to various niche markets. It's a trend which will continue in the days ahead to develop multiple sales channels for books. Savvy authors understand that their books need to be sold in many different places other than bookstores. These authors catch the trend and work hard to open multiple channels to sell their books.

Trend # 5: Competitive Environment for the Small Bookstore Owner

It's well known among publishing personnel that the smaller bookstore owner has a challenging task. Increased competition from the multiple sales channels listed in Trend #4 makes it more difficult for these owners to maintain and grow their business. Many of these retailers are simply closing their doors and getting out of the bookselling business. For example, a number of smaller independent bookstores in New York City have closed their doors in recent years. This is another trend to watch. As someone who wants to write and produce a nonfiction book, you need to be aware of these events.

Trend # 6: Changes in the Book Buying/Decision Making Process

Finally, customers are buying books through catalogs and through package deals. This change in where and how people buy their

books came home to me personally about a year ago. My wife purchased the bestselling *South Beach Diet* book, not in a bookstore but
in a Bed, Bath and Beyond store. I rarely shop in this retail store and
didn't know they sold books. The locations and places books are sold
continue to rapidly change and evolve.

A brief look at these trends will help you start your own journey
to track the various events in the marketplace and how they relate
to book publishing. If you want your book proposal to sell, you
need to continue to be aware of these events.

Would you like to know more ways to speed your success? In the
following chapters, I will tell you 21 secrets. Let's explore them.

Secret #1

Know the Topic of Your Book

**Know the topic of your book and be able to share
this topic in a few words or sentences.**

I COULD FEEL THE INTENSITY increasing among the other
editors involved in acquisitions. I felt it as well because we were fac-
ing a deadline to turn in our material for the next publication board
meeting. We typically set deadlines several weeks in advance of the
actual meeting, then the various participants could read our background materials before the meeting and come prepared with their
questions and comments. Besides the author's proposal, we had
internal documents to get ready for the meeting. An editorial assistant prepared an agenda which gave the order for the editors to present their books for that particular month.

Tensions in our editorial group always tended to run high the day
of the publication board meeting as no one could predict what

would happen in these sessions. There is an old saying about editors that it depends on what they had for breakfast. Reality isn't that subjective but the mood of the room can swing to different extremes. For some meetings, the questions were minimal and the reaction was positive about the authors that I championed for the publishing house.

On other occasions it was different. I walked into the room filled with publishing staff, armed with my stack of folders and paperwork. As an editor, I prepared a series of short presentations on the key details of each book. Another editor on our editorial team had worked at multiple publishing houses and appeared before different groups of these publication boards. This colleague told me, "Our publication board is different and a bit crankier than some of the others."

Waiting for your turn in the room can be a nerve-racking feeling for an editor. Finally my turn came and I walked into the large board room. Key leaders from the publishing house—including sales, marketing and editorial personnel—sat around a conference table. It was almost certain that several of these leaders had only skimmed your paperwork or not read it at all or they read it during your presentation. Some days it was like sitting on the hot seat trying to defend your titles to a room full of skeptics. Other times they were supportive of your selections. As a book is accepted for publication in this meeting, the various groups such as sales and marketing are held responsible for their support of a particular title. Key business decisions for the life and future of the publisher are made in these meetings. You, as the author, aren't present but your view is represented from your work on the book proposal and the voiced words of support from your acquisitions editor.

Your words on your proposal become elevated in importance. How will your book be represented through your words? What is the hook? This should come in the first sentence or two of your overview—the first section for any book proposal. This section defines the topic of your book in a few words. I've already explained the difficulty involved in getting an editor to read your material. Now you have a few seconds to grab the editor's attention. What hook will you use to entice him to keep turning your pages? Your first responsibility is to reach the editor who is thinking about his readers and book buyers when he reads your initial words. He can then use your overview material to hook his publication board.

The overview should be a maximum of one to three pages in length and should clearly explain what the book is about, why it is necessary and what makes this book different than others on the same topic. Normally this material is written in the third person.

If you are looking for a way to concisely tell the idea of your book, I'd suggest that you first write it on paper, but also work with it in an oral format. It's one of the reasons to read your writing aloud after you've finished it—because the ear is less forgiving than the eye. Using this process, you will pick up on all sorts of ways to improve your manuscript.

In the last few years, I've traveled to various parts of the United States and Canada teaching at conferences and meeting with potential authors at 15-minute appointments. Some authors are deathly frightened of these meetings. I suggest they take a deep breath and relax, then enter these meetings without fear. Editors are merely regular people who have specialized information about their particular publishing needs.

At some of these conferences, I've had as many as 50 of these 15–minute pitch sessions over a few days. Toward the end of these intense meetings, it's difficult for me to absorb any new ideas but it's how a particular conference is set up. Many times a potential author who is obviously unprepared will consume the entire 15 minutes to explain a nonfiction book concept. Words like hook or pitch for the reader aren't in their vocabulary. They have not formulated a concise way to explain their idea in a few minutes.

I recommend every writer to prepare three levels of pitches:

1. One sentence: Develop a one sentence pitch which gives the key message of your nonfiction book.

2. One paragraph: Develop a paragraph pitch for your book that leaves the editor wanting to know more, or something that will stimulate questions from the editor for more information.

3. The page overview: Develop a one to three page overview of your topic that will be a key part of your book proposal.

The following simple outline format will give you a framework for writing your overview and pitch for the editor:

1. Hook the editor with a strong opening statement that will quickly bring attention to your particular topic. This takes work and effort to put together an effective sentence that can be shocking, surprising, humorous or an attention-getting fact.

2. Now hold the editor's attention with some additional information to keep him reading and to keep his focus on your particular topic.

3. Next, sell the editor on the idea and the importance of this topic for their publishing house. Do some research and know what you are talking about. Back your ideas up with statistics.

4. Then sell yourself. Tell why you are the best and only person to write this material for the publisher. Hint at this answer in your overview materials.

5. Finally, make sure you are focused on a single book idea rather than proposing several different books in the overview. It's important to stay focused with nonfiction and not stray too far from your selected topic.

This hook for the editor and the book overview may be the most significant part of your proposal. In succinct language, you are pitching the essence of your idea. Why is this element the most important feature? For the answer, let's return to the publication board meeting where your acquisitions editor is pitching your project to the publishing team. You aren't in the room but for a moment, pretend you are an invisible observer in the corner watching the meeting.

I've finally gotten my turn to present my various projects and your nonfiction idea is the first one I present. I take your hook or the first few sentences of your overview and those words introduce my presentation about your topic. In abbreviated terms, I explain the need for your book, then how your well-written book will fill this particular need. Next I show the sales and marketing team how your idea is a perfect fit with the types of books we publish, yet it makes an original contribution to the literature on this topic. It's a delicate balance of presentation from the editor showing how your nonfiction book fills a need in the marketplace and why you are the absolute best person to write this particular book.

The participants in the room are naturally skeptical. They need books to fill their list and have a certain number of books for each season, yet it's also important to invest their limited financial resources in the *right* books. For example, parenting books were one of our areas of acquisitions at the publishing house. The problem with a parenting book is the crowded number of best-selling backlist books already in this area. If I proposed a parenting book from an unknown author, it would have to fill a unique niche to compete and actually get sold into this market.

Some books are tossed off the agenda and the consideration process with a comment from sales or the president of the publishing house. If the vice president of sales says he can't place a particular book, his comment will turn everyone else at the table against the product. The various members of the publication board will make a note on their agenda to vote "no" and move on to the next book.

There are common reasons for a book to be rejected in the publication board meeting.

• Too much competition in that particular market. The marketing person may know about a forthcoming book that, as the editor, I didn't know about. If a major author in the market is coming out with a title, it will limit an unknown author with a similar idea. Several people have suggested to me that any book with the word "purpose" or talking about a "life theme" or "life direction" has been rejected in the current marketplace because of Rick Warren's best-selling *Purpose Driven Life*. I have no proof of this limitation but it gives you an idea of what can keep your idea from being published.

- That particular idea has been already been done. While the author (and the editor) prepare possible competitive titles to a proposed book, if someone suggests a best-selling or steady backlist book on the same idea, it will keep your proposed idea from going forward into a published book.

- That particular idea has *never* been done before. Authors who propose a particular niche or audience for a book need to know if the members of this audience buy books or if there is a way to reach them? If the sales and marketing people answer "no," then the project will be rejected.

- The idea is too expensive to produce. This type of situation often occurs with children's books. An author will propose a "gimmick" for the book such as cutting the book into a shape. This additional step in the process will increase production costs and cause the publishing team to reject the idea.

As an acquisitions editor, I was doing well if 50 percent of my books were approved to be contracted. Sometimes I would propose eight books and get only one or two approvals.

As the author of the nonfiction book proposal, you have the responsibility to hook the reader, hook the editor and hook other people within the publishing house. You will not be present at this meeting, yet your overview provides a key tool for the editor to win the necessary approval. Don't send your editor into the fray unarmed. Work hard on the overview section of your proposal.

Secret #2

Know the Audience for Your Book

Understand some specifics about who will read your book.

IMAGINE YOUR BOOK IS already written and shelved in the local bookstore. In which section will it appear? What type of customer will walk over there, read the back cover and then purchase the book?

I have reviewed numerous proposals which proclaim, "This book is for everyone." The experience has made me a bit jaded on this topic. Every book is not for every person. Thus, this next step involves research. Who buys books and what type of bookstores or locations for books (such as general merchandise stores) would carry your book?

Everyone who writes books should ask him or herself, Are you counting on a large volume of men to read your book? The average man reads two books a year. Women purchase about 70 percent of all books and 46 percent of paperbacks. The bulk of the market is slanted toward women. Most people outside of publishing don't consider that fact, but think about it the next time you walk into a large bookstore. How are the displays and the books positioned? Are they aimed toward men or women?

If you are proposing a book targeted for men, you need to show in your proposal how you will reach this audience with your book idea. Then the publisher will have to decide if they have an entrance to reach this particular market. Many publishers have tried to reach men with books and failed miserably, sustaining a large financial cost. You are going to have to convince the editor that you know your audience and that you can reach this particular audience with your message.

A literary agent once told me about a book written by a popular skateboarder that she struggled to sell. Publisher after publisher rejected the book because they couldn't see the potential market for it. Finally the agent sold the book to a well-known publishing imprint. This publisher saw the market and the book sold over 16,000 hardcover copies during the first year for a respectable result. Part of your challenge as an author is convincing a publisher about your audience and that it is reachable.

Reaching your audience is not the only issue. Here's another one to consider: If the audience is a specialized niche, do you have special access? For example, you are a counselor writing a nonfiction book proposal to help children of alcoholic parents. It's a good credential that you are one of 10,000 members of the American Association of Christian Counselors (AACC). The question is, Do you have special access to Dr. Tim Clinton, the president of AACC? If so, do you have some measure of influence over Dr. Clinton so he could use your book as a membership renewal incentive (i.e., he would take 10,000 copies of your book)? This would be a special incentive for a publisher to consider and accept your proposal. You need to carefully weigh your audience and how you will take the time and energy to reach this audience with your proposed book.

While every book is not for every person on the planet, the audience for your book has to be large enough to merit publishing the book. If your audience is too small, the publisher will reject the book. If your audience isn't appropriate for that publisher, they will reject the book. Or if the audience isn't one that publisher believes they can easily reach, they will reject the proposal. It's really pretty simple.

In one publication board meeting I championed a devotional book for senior citizens. The author's proposal included some innovative ideas for markets such as hospital gift shops and other places. The publishing executives recognized the growing number of senior citizens in the U.S., yet they wondered if seniors read books. Then, much more important, they wondered if seniors purchased books. My superiors also speculated about the size of the audience who purchased books for seniors. They didn't have any immediate answers to these questions so they rejected the proposal and went on to the next book on their agenda. As an author, you want to provide all of the ammunition possible in your proposal to pinpoint the audience and the ability to sell books to this audience.

Having detailed information about your audience is a secret worth knowing and including in your proposal. And if you have that sentence, "This book is for everyone" or some variation of it, delete it from your proposal and go to work to make it more specific. This research and audience identification will pay off in the eyes of the acquisitions editor, as well as with others within the publishing house.

Secret #3

Understand What Each Chapter Will Contain

Understand and write a chapter by chapter summary.

THIS SECTION OF THE BOOK PROPOSAL is more important than the book manuscript in your search to obtain a nonfiction publishing contract. As the author, you have to determine what each chapter will contain and the unique focus of these chapters to meet the expectations and needs of your audience.

I was talking with a high profile Christian artist who has numerous celebrity friends that will write endorsements and a foreword for the book. The publisher will certainly be enticed to seriously consider a book proposal from this artist as a result of the celebrity friends that will be involved. As I talked with this artist, I pulled him up short. "Yes, these names will help us get the publisher's attention, but here's the critical question: What topic will this book address?" I have no doubt that this artist can tell fascinating stories, but when the publishing executives come down to making a decision, the kingpin will be the contents of this chapter-by-chapter summary. The sample writing also will be an important consideration factor, but the decision makers will study these summary paragraphs. Make sure you put lots of energy and effort into this section of your proposal.

Because nonfiction books are rarely completely written, the chapter-by-chapter summary is an important element to show the editor, along with others, that you understand the direction and the overall flow of your book's content. From my years of creating these types of nonfiction proposals, rarely has an editor reorganized my sections or changed any of this content. The summary clearly shows where I'm going overall. In general, I write from a brief outline and the chapter-by-chapter summary contains the added benefit for the writer. It will provide you a roadmap when you write the book.

Divide the research into different groups or categories based on your preliminary research. If the topic falls into only four or five categories, then divide them further into sub-groups. These divisions are the beginnings of your various chapters in the book. Almost every nonfiction book contains 10 to 12 chapters, some as many as 16 to 20. If your book falls into the latter category, group your chapters into three or four major parts or sections.

There are at least six different ways to organize a nonfiction book.

- Chronological order
- In order of increasing or decreasing importance or complexity
- Order of need
- Classification and division
- Inductive and deductive
- Literary order

No matter which format you select, make sure your first chapter will hook the reader and hold their attention. This chapter needs to stress the benefits and rewards for anyone who buys this book.

I'll say more about the sample later, but your first chapter should be compelling for the reader.

Like the title for your book, chapter titles give you another opportunity to add creativity and pizzazz to your book proposal. Select titles that reflect your method of book organization, but which are also catchy to continually hook the reader (the editor).

Now, you have created your overall outline and essentially a table of contents that lists your chapter titles in a specific order of presentation. What will each of these chapters contain?

You can write these chapter summaries in complete sentences or they can be written in sentence fragments containing an active verb. Examples of active verbs to include in chapter summaries could be: explains, suggests, defines, shows, ends with, discusses, introduces, lists, offers, details, features, draws, gives, presents and advises.

Each chapter summary should include the topics of your book in specific terms that include facts, figures, statistics, dates, name terms, people and concepts.

These summaries should be limited to a paragraph or at the most two paragraphs. If you write much more than these limited words, you risk writing the entire chapter instead of the summary. The editor needs to see only the overall flow of your book and a summary of the chapter material.

Some steps to writing excellent chapter summaries could include:

- Minimize the use of "This chapter…" and "Readers will…"
- Avoid weak beginnings to your sentence such as "It is" and "There is."
- Vary your sentences in terms of types and length.
- Use active verbs and reduce the use of "to be" verbs such as is/was/were.
- Include specific topics, facts and terms.
- Include at least one specific feature and one clear benefit for the reader.

- Limit summaries to two paragraphs, but make sure these short summaries contain enough specific topics to merit a well-defined chapter.

The chapter summary is a key part of your book proposal and will require some effort to pull together the information that you need. Don't shy away from this hard work because it will pay off in the long run as an editor reads and loves the work you've done on this book proposal.

Secret #4

Understand Why You Are the Author

Understand and explain your credentials for writing this book.

WHY ARE YOU THE BEST possible person to write this particular nonfiction book? When you write this section, don't be shy. It's the time to roll out your authority and credibility. Publishers give increasing importance to the author and their connections in their particular area of expertise. Six key areas should be included in this biographical sketch:

- What are your credentials in this particular subject area?
- What are your career credentials to write about this topic? Begin with your most professional credentials related to the topic, then list other careers in descending order of importance.
- What is your educational background to write on this topic? In general, a masters degree and higher carries weight independent of the subject area, although some agents and editors avoid academicians

and their writing. Academic writing is completely different than the popular type of writing which is most broadly published. Often someone steeped in academia has learned to write in convoluted sentences and difficult syntax. If you have a higher degree in a particular area related to your topic, it can help you if your writing does not sound like a textbook. Be aware that touting a higher degree can send a message that the editor or agent should be cautious.

- What credits, awards, publications and memberships can you highlight that relate to your topic? If you have published in magazines, then list some of them, particularly if the titles are familiar to the editor or agent. Leave out anything that would diminish your proposed work or you as the author.

- What promotional skills have you shown through your past books or publications? Not everyone has something to put in this area so don't panic if nothing comes to mind here. If you have had success promoting other products, be sure to include them in this section.

- What personal data can you include? Some authors choose to leave off this final section, but it's the one paragraph or opportunity for the author to show that they are an interesting human being—someone that the editor (or agent) would like to meet. This personal information will separate you from a mass of qualifications and credentials the editor sorts through as he or she makes a decision about an author.

Editors and agents will appreciate the energy and effort that you pour into this section of your proposal.

Secret #5

Know Your Competition

As the author, it is your responsibility to research and know the competition to your proposed book.

AFTER REVIEWING COUNTLESS proposals, you would be shocked at the large number of beginning authors who include a competition section that begins, "This idea has no competition because it is unique and has never been done before." Or they say, "There is nothing like this in the marketplace. No competition." Wrong. If you have this type of language in your proposal, remove it. The acquisitions editor or literary agent will know that you are an amateur who has no real sense about the realities of the book publishing marketplace.

While your material is unique and will fill an exclusive unique place in the market, *every new book will compete with other books.* King Solomon had it right when he wrote, "there's no end to the publishing of books" (Ecclesiastes 12:12 *The Message*).

You are the expert on your particular nonfiction topic, so it's important that you include which books will compete with your product. I often tell writers to imagine their book in the bookstore. Which section of the bookstore will contain your book? Now think about the books that will be next to your book. Who are these authors and what will make a customer select your book instead of a competitor's?

In this section, you need to list half a dozen books that will be direct competition to your proposed book. In particular, make sure you examine the bestselling books in your specific category such as self-help or religion. Now, here's the key: Explain how your book is different and distinct from these books. Give a one or two sentence summary of the contents of the competing book, then a couple of sentences about how your book is different.

Many writers are surprised to learn that researching the competition is the responsibility of the author, not the publisher. No editor can be an expert in every aspect of the book market. You are the author who is asking the publisher to invest in your proposal—so you have the obligation to locate your competition, understand the content of the competition, then distinguish those books from the new product you propose.

When you list the competition, make sure you list the title of the competing book, the author, the publisher and the publication year. Many authors neglect at least one of these aspects in their competition section of the book proposal. As an editor, I would have to ask them to revise their proposal and include it. To make this request, I had to locate a phone number or email address for the author (your proposal should include both elements), ask for the additional information and give them a deadline. To make these types of requests require the editor's time which is in short supply. This lack also gives your proposal another reason for that dreaded form rejection letter.

As the writer, you may never know the true reason your proposal was rejected; thus, your objective should be to "rejection proof" your nonfiction book proposal and eliminate this type of simple omission.

If a particular competing product has been on the bestseller list or has sold many copies and you have this information, then include it in this section about the competition. Such information will affirm your expertise in the topic for the editor (or agent).

Secret #6

Cast a Vision of Your Book

Understand the length, size and shape of your proposed book.

As THE WRITER OF THE PROPOSAL (and eventually the book), it is your responsibility—not the editor's or publisher's—to create the basic vision for the book. It's much easier to change a suggested format or length than to create it in the first place.

Many people fail to include this specific information in their nonfiction book proposals. What does your book look like? Is it 40,000 words or 140,000 words? When I've called authors and asked for this information, they often reply, "Well, what size of book do you need?" As an editor, I hesitate to give this size or cast this vision. I've been a writer for too many years and know that whatever vision I would cast, the author would tell me, "That's exactly what I was thinking," whether they were thinking such a thing or not, because of their eagerness to sell the manuscript.

It is the responsibility of the author to cast the vision for the book and project a word count and finished length. To help you cast this vision, let me tell you that most standard 192-page paperback books are about 50,000 to 60,000 words. (This book is 42,000 words.) Many beginning writers are hesitant to give such a number because they've never written a long book. Others include a smaller number like 25,000 or 30,000 words. This size is not attractive to many publishers as it produces a small book with a thin thickness.

Why is the thickness a factor? Walk into any bookstore and look specifically at the number of books displayed with the cover face out on the bookshelf. You'll find only a few. It's mostly a space issue with the bookstore owner. More books can be stocked if they are spine out from the bookshelf. A 25,000-word nonfiction book will not have much of a presence in the store with the spine out and it will easily be lost on the shelf.

Some authors will propose a spiral-bound book so the reader can fold the book back into a smaller space to write inside the book. These authors are attempting to create a useful book for the reader which is admirable, but they are not thinking about the actual retail sales for their book. Where is the spine on a spiral-bound book? If you are considering this type of binding, I recommend you go to your local bookstore and search for spiral-bound books. I suspect you will rarely find them except in the cookbook section. Marketing potential is lost with a spiral-bound book. If your proposal calls for this type of binding, you limit the number of publishers who can consider your project or you may have to go to a specific publisher.

Your proposed vision for the book should be something a large number of publishers could produce. When many unpublished writers envision a book, they include blank sections for the reader to answer questions from a study guide. These inexperienced writers believe these blank pages will attract readers and make their book more interactive. Such thinking is wrong under most circumstances. How many pages will be added to the book to accomplish this "interactive section"?

From the publisher's perspective, the increased page count only raises the production costs and the final retail price of the book. Is it worth this additional cost? In the majority of cases, the publisher will say "no" and reject your book. If they are interested in the concept of the proposal, however, they will work with you to see if they can eliminate the interactive portion. As the author, you want to rejection proof your proposal from such issues and think about how such details will appear to the publisher. Don't give the publisher a simple reason to reject your entire proposal because you've proposed a spiral-bound book.

Many writers tell me, "I want the publisher to decide how big the book will be." Then they say with pride, "I'm flexible." To be "flexible" will not cut it with the editor. You are the expert on this particular topic and subject matter; it's why the publisher is paying you an advance and investing a great deal of money to produce your book. You have a responsibility to envision the length of your book. How many words will you need to completely cover your selected topic?

This number is critical to a successful book proposal as the editor uses this proposed word count to project the number of pages in the published book. Then he works with the production personnel to run the production numbers. These numbers are put into the Performa or spreadsheet document that gives the complete financials on the book. The author never sees these numbers, but based on these figures, the editor has parameters for offering an advance on the royalties of the book and the percentage for royalties.

Without the author's word count, the editor can't accomplish this important function—or he takes a wild guess at the number which could be substantially wrong. These financial figures are used for much more than simply your project inside the publishing house. They are used for annual budget projections for the editorial area and other places. While seemingly a small issue, these financials figure into other areas inside the publishing house.

Beyond the word count or length of the manuscript, you also need to provide a delivery date. It is important to remember the word count with nonfiction because the entire manuscript is not complete. You have written only the proposal and a chapter or two of the project. How long will it take you to write the remainder of the book?

When I have approached authors about this question, they ask me, "When do you need my manuscript?" It's a trick question that your editor cannot answer for you. You are the only person who knows the demands on your time and energy during the coming months and how quickly you can write the book. This timeframe is different for every person because one person writes several thousand words in a day while others may only be able to write several hundred words a day.

One of my author friends regularly writes books that appear on the *New York Times* bestseller list. Because he has written many books, he knows that he can produce a publishable manuscript in 21 days of hard work. He thrives on this challenge. Most authors would crumble under this volume of words because of their speaking schedule or their day job, and they may need a year or even 18 months to write the manuscript.

Why is the completion date important? Because whatever date you tell the editor for completion will go into your book contract. This date sets off a chain of events throughout the publishing house (production, marketing, sales and editorial). A detailed schedule of events and benchmarks to produce the book is created and various people are held accountable for the scheduled events—events that are unknown to the authors. Authors are notoriously late; however, a late manuscript can cause delays that could hinder the success of your book.

For example, who will be editing your book when it comes into the publishing house? It may be an inside person, or the publishing house may send your book to an outside freelance editor.

When I worked as an aquisitions editor, our managing editor determined that an author needed a developmental editor to work with her from the beginning of the project. The publishing house leadership was excited about this author and wanted the book to be excellent. I began to call my network of editors looking for someone to do it and to negotiate a timeframe and price for the editing.

For my first call, I connected with one of the top freelance editors in the business whom I have known many years. She regularly edits some best-selling authors who have sold millions of copies. Her first question was "When will this project begin?" I explained the manuscript was due in a few weeks. She instantly said, "My schedule is booked solid for the next year."

My reaction was incredible since I didn't know what I was doing next month. "You're booked for a year?"

Then she explained, "Yes, usually I am contracted at the same time the author is contracted." When I called some other freelance editors, I learned the same story from them—their schedules couldn't accommodate this book that needed developmental editing because it was planned 12 months in advance.

Let's return to the topic of casting a vision for your book and knowing when you will deliver the manuscript. If during the contract process, you agree to submit your manuscript in six months or eight months or twelve months, then your editor will be expecting your manuscript *on time*. If you deliver your manuscript a month late or two months late (it happens more often than you would know), you will throw off all the internal plans the publishing house is making for your book, plus the assigned freelance editor will have their schedule thrown off. You will set off a chain reaction that can and will influence the effectiveness of your book sales.

Also, the marketing will be affected regarding your manuscript delivery date. The publishing world has several trade magazines such as *Publisher's Weekly*, *CBA Marketplace* and *Christian Retailing*. Each of these publications has a slightly different audience, but they all select books to be reviewed and highlighted to booksellers (always an important market for authors). The submission deadlines are months in advance of the release date for a review of your book to appear in these key trade magazines. If your publisher doesn't have your manuscript, then your book will not be one of those submitted to the trade magazines for review and you will miss a key marketing opportunity. Almost every magazine is working four to six months in advance of the cover date printed on the magazine. The marketing department of your publisher is aware of these due dates and needs to have your book manuscript in order to make the greatest possible impact.

You don't want to bear the responsibility of your book not being properly marketed or sold into the stores because you missed your book deadline by a month or two or three. Be thoughtful about it and don't give yourself a deadline for delivery that will be impossible to achieve. Set a reasonable due date which will work for you. It's a key part of your responsibility with the vision casting for your book.

Secret #7

Create a Dynamic and Fascinating Marketing Plan

Show the publisher that you understand the marketing for your book and your willingness to be involved.

MANY WOULD-BE AUTHORS are surprised to see this element in the component of an excellent nonfiction book proposal. They think to themselves (and some of them verbalize), "I'm not self-publishing my book. Isn't the publisher supposed to be putting together a market plan with a specific commitment of dollars?"

Here's the problem: Every publisher has limited marketing and publicity dollars to promote their list of books. The bulk of the money will go to the top authors, and if you are a new author, you can expect that your book will receive a minimal treatment—unless you show the publisher that you deserve something different.

I met Jacqueline Deval, publisher at Hearst Books, who has also been a director of publicity at several publishing houses. One of the best resources for authors is Deval's book called *Publicize Your Book!, An Insider's Guide to Getting Your Book the Attention It Deserves* (Perigee Books, 2003) http://snipurl.com/pubyb. From the opening paragraph, Deval provides authors with the following realistic expectation:

> The reality of book publishing is that there are too few resources to support every book. This means that some books will get publicity campaigns and budgets while others will go without. Additionally, most publishing houses are not staffed with enough publicists to mount a full-fledged campaign for every book. Because of this, editors must compete with one another to lobby the publisher, and the marketing and publicity departments, for the funds and staff attention to promote their books.

What type of marketing ammunition can you include in your non-fiction book proposal so your editor can champion your cause? Because of the expense of publishing a book, a publisher will expect you to actively work at marketing your book to your connections. Many writers are stumped about what to include in this section of their proposals so they write, "I'm willing to do radio, television and print interviews to promote my book." Of course, you will be willing to do these interviews. If not, you have no business even taking the steps of creating a book proposal and writing a book. Publicizing your book comes with the territory after the book is published. Other authors will write, "My book should be featured on Oprah." Every publisher longs for their books to be featured on Oprah because this event drives books to the bestseller list. The reality is few authors get this opportunity—even though their publisher may try. The producers at the Oprah television show are bombarded with literally thousands of new books. It's not realistic to include such plans in your proposal.

To achieve success in your marketing plan, you need to get into a different mind-set. As Deval says in the first chapter,

> An author who thinks like a marketer, and who starts thinking about marketing before the book is even completed, will help the book toward a successful publication. The author is in the best position to offer suggestions for marketing that the house might have overlooked and sometimes to help bridge any difficult internal relationships among the publishing team that might impede the book's success. (In-house squabbles do happen in the business, and while in a just world they shouldn't interfere with a book's progress, sometimes they do.) Most important, the author can be the catalyst to motivate a house's enthusiasm about a book (page 4).

Deval's perspective in her book is valuable to anyone writing a nonfiction book proposal or with a book to be published. As an insider, she understands the stresses and limitations within a publisher. She helps the author come alongside the publisher with creative and cost-effective ideas without being a pushy, high maintenance author (yes, they exist).

Take some time to creatively think about the topic and the book that you propose. Which specialty groups are potential targets for this book? Do you have a connection to these markets through an organization or network to reach them with your book? If you don't presently have a connection with the target group, how can you acquire one ? You have the passion and drive for your particular topic, and you need to pass this passion on to the publisher.

Can you come up with a special market for your book that will sell 10,000 to 100,000 copies from the first printing? Does this sound impossible? It's not. According to Jerrold Jenkins, president of the Jenkins Group in Traverse City, Michigan, the majority of special sales (a special sale is anything outside of the traditional bookstore setting) for books originate from the author who turns up these leads and creative ideas to sell thousands of books. Could your book contain a special back cover with the symbol of the organization and be used as a membership renewal gift? Could it contain a special letter from the president on the first page of the book? These books with a special cover or special inserted letter are called "special sales."

Book sales have a fundamental problem that has been around since the Great Depression. Retailers can order your book into the stores (good news for that to happen). But it doesn't remain on their book shelves forever. If your book doesn't sell after a period of time, they can return the book to the publisher (not good news). These returns are charged against the earnings of your royalties. Special sales are never returned! They are guaranteed sales for the publisher and the author. I would encourage you to take some time at the Jenkins Group website (http://snipurl.com/jenkins) and study the various examples of special sales. While these examples might not be exactly like your idea, be creative in your plan and potential for sales and include this plan into your proposal under the category of promotion.

As an acquisitions editor, I love to locate an author who understands it takes more than excellent writing to sell large volumes of their book. I've discovered a book that is a valuable resource for writers in this area called *Beyond the Bookstore, How to Sell More Books Profitably to Non-Bookstore Markets* by Brian Jud (Reed Business Press, 2004). http://snipurl.com/btbks This book documents that more than half of the books sold are sold through non-traditional channels such as mail order, warehouse clubs and other means.

Have you ever read the sales numbers of a particular book and wondered how *that* particular book ever sold in the bookstore? Some of those big sales numbers have been outside the bookstore.

Beyond the Bookstore is a valuable resource for any writer to think outside the box. Jud covers 79 specific strategies for generating special sales. As you read these strategies, determine which ideas are appropriate for your book, then incorporate these ideas into your nonfiction or fiction book proposal. Including this type of information at the beginning of the publishing process will show your publisher your intention to be proactive in the sales process. Proactive authors who understand how to sell books are attractive authors to any publisher.

Reed Business also produces *Publisher's Weekly* which is loaded with current statistics and contact information such as, "Today, the worldwide book market approximates $90 billion. Almost one third of those sales occur in the United States. Over the past ten years, the amount of sales through traditional outlets is decreased by 11 per cent (down 19 per cent without factoring Internet sales), and sales through non-bookstore outlets have increased by 8 per cent."

Three major advantages of special sales include control over your destiny, customization potential and nontraditional market segmentation. As an additional resource, this book includes a CD-ROM to help generate a marketing plan and give the right emphasis for each market channel. Using this book and CD package to generate a detailed marketing plan for your nonfiction book proposal will help your proposal stand out from all the others on the acquisitions editor's desk. Only the author has the passion and intense interest in their book. Use this book to increase your sales and strengthen your book proposals.

If you include even the beginnings of an effective marketing plan in your proposal, you send the following messages to the publisher.

1. You are someone who thinks about marketing and is eager to partner with the publisher to gain sales for your book.

2. You've effectively come alongside as a partner and colleague to the marketing personnel of the publishing house.

3. You've positioned your proposal as different and distinct from the many proposals which will not include this effort—and as a result your proposal is much more attractive to the publishing executives and something they should publish.

Never forget that there are thousands of proposals circulating at a publisher. Your goal is to make your proposal irresistible—and something they have to publish—before a competitor snaps it up.

Secret #8

Write a Spellbinding Sample Chapter

**Your sample chapter must be compelling because
it is a taste of what the rest will become.**

WHEN I PRESENTED a nonfiction book proposal at the publishing house, several of the executives didn't read the first part of the proposal that included the overview, chapter summaries, author bio or the marketing plan. Instead, they turned to the sample chapter and read it first. If the sample was excellent, they read the rest of the proposal. If the sample was poor, then they had formed their opinion (and likely a final decision) regarding the suitability of this book to add to our publishing list.

In many ways, this type of reading pattern is smart—because the writing should be what sells the publishing executive on a particular project. It's why they *have* to publish your particular project, so make sure you invest a substantial amount of energy and excellence into the writing. It should be compelling and the stories should make the reader (editor) turn the page to learn more. You need a combination of personal experience and how-to information in a nonfiction book that is appropriate for the particular publishing house.

And what are you adding "extra" to the sample chapter? Beyond your storytelling (which needs to be excellent) and your information (which needs to be simple, yet profound), are you adding some questions for the reader to think about or sidebar articles to give additional tidbits of information throughout the book? What special feature can you add that will make your book stand out?

Here's one caution as you add this "extra" feature to your sample chapter: Make sure you consider the cost of this feature. Sometimes authors will create a plastic "gimmick" to go with the book without thinking how this "gimmick" will be produced and what it will add to the value of the book? If the feature is something that can be printed like the rest of the book, it will not be an issue. But if it involves artwork (read extra cost for the publisher) or design work (again more production cost), then your "extra" may be a cause for rejection rather than help your proposal.

Children's authors tend to lean more toward using gimmicks. I once met with a new author who was also an artist. She had produced a series of removable Christmas tree ornaments in a book format that would celebrate the days leading up to Christmas. While the concept was interesting, the production costs would be astronomical. This author looked at me like I was crazy when I asked, "And what will be the retail price of this book? A hundred dollars?" I'm certain she thought I was trying to blow off her idea, but I was simply trying to get her to realize the cost of such a feature. The idea wasn't a practical one that a publisher could execute without a high retail cost or a huge volume of printing.

You may have noticed that best-selling authors' books have some very nice features. Possibly beautiful artwork or the author's signature is embossed into the hardcover underneath the paper book jacket. These features are possible if you are going to print two million copies at the same time and are able to gain strong economic discounts and economy of scale. In most cases, however, new authors can't ask or expect such features as the publisher will be taking enough of a risk in simply printing their book. Adding the "extra" feature has to pay off for the publisher.

Take extra time to polish your sample chapter so every member of the publishing committee will be eager to get your book under contract and a part of their forthcoming publishing plans. This is something you *can* do as the author to help build enthusiasm inside and outside of the publishing house.

Secret #9:

Keep the Title and Format Simple

Propose a short, catchy title and a standard format.

THE TITLE FOR YOUR BOOK should be three to five words that snap the editor's head around and hook them into reading your proposal. It should also tell the editors what the book is about.

Many first time authors are concerned when they read the standard book contract which normally says the publisher selects the title for the book. If you have a great deal of personal attachment to your own idea for a book title, I'd encourage you to get over it. As I said in the previous secret, the book publisher has a far greater financial investment in the actual production costs of the book; thus, he is the final authority on the title. I always tell beginning writers that if you create a great title, it will stick throughout the consideration process.

As you write your nonfiction book proposal to sell, your task is to find the perfect title for your book—along with several alternative titles.

For example, I created the title *Lessons from the Pit* for our original book proposal that eventually received a book contract. The publisher added a lengthy subtitle but the original short title stuck throughout the entire process.

Many times I've created the title for my book and it's been ultimately used—even though in my contract I gave the final authority over to the publisher. In particular, my nonfiction children's book titles have remained the same. For one of these books, I wrote a short retold Bible story about Paul and Silas in jail entitled *A Strange Place to Sing*. You have to admit that singing when you are thrown into jail is a strange reaction, but it's exactly what the apostle Paul and his traveling companion Silas did in the book of Acts. A short story about Jesus and the children was titled *Never Too Busy*. This title illustrated the central theme that Jesus Christ is never too busy for a child (or an adult). Simple titles usually will stay throughout the entire publishing process—particularly if they are central to the content of your book.

Another factor to consider in choosing titles is whether any other book already has this or a similar title. The book publisher will look at your title with this perspective in mind. It doesn't make sense for salesmen to present a new book to a retailer, only to have the retailer say, "Isn't that like this book over here?" Because you can't copyright a title, two different publishers can issue a book with the exact same title.

I found an example of this in the fiction area. (It also happens in nonfiction.) One of the popular genres of fiction is called "Chick Lit." Kristen Billerbeck's novel, *What A Girl Wants* (WestBow Press), was released March 7, 2004, in an original paperback. Later, while reading a monthly newsletter at a Border's bookstore, I spotted the same title—from a different author and a different publisher—*What A Girl Wants* by Liz Maverick—a paperback novel released on March 2, 2004, by NAL Trade. As much as possible, publishers attempt to avoid this confusing situation.

Even without the same title, you can count on readers to confuse your book title and sometimes recall a wrong word or two. Yet you still want the retailer to be able to locate your book and sell it. Put the necessary time and energy into researching and creating an excellent title, but offer several alternative titles as well.

Book publishing is not a solitary task; rather, it is a matter of consensus building. As the author, you have to convince an editor to believe in your book and champion it internally. This editor then has to convince a room full of publishing executives that they need to publish your book. In the title process, give your editor the ammunition he needs to convince the others. An excellent title is a factor you need to consider thoughtfully *before* you submit your proposal.

Do not send your submission electronically unless the editor specifically requests it. In trying to cut costs, many writers prefer to submit their proposals via email attachment, but most editors *do not* prefer this format. They receive a great deal of email from their authors and publishing colleagues and other people inside and outside of their company. One publishing executive told me that he receives over 300 emails *a day*. Because this executive occasionally travels and doesn't check his email for several days, you can imagine the backlog of information he must wade through upon his return. The same situation is true for editors and agents. Many publishers have stopped accepting unsolicited proposals and manuscripts due to the overwhelming flood of poor proposals.

As someone submitting a nonfiction book proposal, you want to remain above this fray. Don't send a book proposal via email unless you first secure permission from the editor. In these times of computer viruses, editors are hesitant to open an attachment from someone they don't know. Your time and energy will be wasted trying to use an electronic submission process.

Another no-no: When you mail your final book proposal, do not use colored paper or fancy fonts. No one wants to read material in Bookman Old Style or Lucinda Sans Typewriter—even if your computer has these fonts. You would be surprised at the lengths some people go to get attention with their mailed manuscript. These writers get attention but it's the negative type. Stick to something standard such as 12 point New Times Roman font.

Also, there is no need to put your proposal in a three-ring binder or use any extra folders or presentation materials. I once received a large manuscript in a notebook binder. The author had punched three holes into every single page of the manuscript, then placed it into the binder and shipped it overnight to my address.

There is no need to include your graduation certificates or your PowerPoint presentations (yes, people send these items to publishers. I've seen it firsthand). Also you don't have to send your proposal by priority mail, Federal Express or overnight delivery. Some people send proposals using this method so they can track it and know that it has arrived on the editor's desk. This is an unnecessary expense.

While it is completely obvious to me, I need to tell you that your manuscript must be typed. I had always heard about handwritten manuscripts but despite the hundreds I have reviewed, I had never seen one—until recently. I received an entirely handwritten manuscript (fiction). I found it almost frightening to be holding the single copy of another person's work—especially in this electronic world. I read it and returned it promptly to the author so it did not stay long in my possession. Most of my recent book contracts will say that the manuscript is to be delivered to the publisher in an electronic format to save keyboard time. The overall key point is for your submission to be professional and normal—not to stand out because of something unusual. It is your concept, your writing and your storytelling that will make the greatest difference to the editor.

As I've explained earlier in this book, the editor has many other tasks and will not read your material any faster if it is sent overnight.

This may gain you a negative reaction instead of a positive one. Only send something rapidly if you have been in touch with the editor in advance and they request it. Otherwise, stick to regular mail and put your proposal on plain white paper.

Secret #10

Get High Profile Endorsements

High profile endorsements or a foreword from a well-known expert can make a difference.

DO YOU KNOW A WELL-KNOWN PERSON who will agree to write an endorsement or foreword for your book? Resist saying that you will seek endorsements from Billy Graham, Max Lucado or President George Bush—unless, of course, you have personal access to these people. Well-known public figures are besieged for endorsements and forewords. Several of my best-selling author friends receive requests such as these each week from publishers and their author friends. If they receive these requests, you can imagine how difficult it would be for an unknown person to receive an endorsement.

Most of these people will want to read the entire book manuscript before associating their name with it because of poor experiences in the past. Others will just reject you up front and still others are prohibited from endorsing or writing forewords for books by their nonprofit boards.

As an editor, I'm almost cynically amused when I receive a proposal from an author who suggests endorsements from Dr. James Dobson at Focus on the Family, Billy Graham and other well-known figures with whom they have no relationship or means to get such an endorsement. Yet in some cases with a completely unknown author, I've seen publishing executives vote to publish a book because the proposal included a foreword from a well-known Bible college professor or someone else with instant recognition. If you can collect such a foreword, include this information in your proposal. Make sure this person is well-known in the broadest possible circles of influence. Some beginning authors include endorsements from their local pastor who is virtually unknown. It's better to omit these types of endorsements from unknown people as it brands you as an amateur.

One of the best articles I recommend to writers in this area is an article titled, *The Elder Rage Success Sage* written by Jacqueline Marcell (http://snipurl.com/Elder). An unpublished author, Marcell collected *57 rejections* with her book manuscript. She decided the only way publishers would seriously consider her topic was to gather numerous celebrity endorsements *before* the manuscript was contracted. After nine months of work, she had impressive quotes from celebrities such as Hugh Downs, Leeza Gibbons, Dr. John Gray, Mark Victor Hansen, Art Linkletter and many others. As she writes in this article, "Polite persistence turned out to be the key."

Think about the potential reader for your book. What person's endorsement would influence that reader to purchase the book? With this list in hand, can you possibly reach this person and get an endorsement?

This article shows the power of persistence. Sometimes you will not receive an endorsement simply because you didn't ask. Make sure you allow several months for the person to meet your request. If you expect the endorsement or forward to be completed in a few days, you are bound to get the easiest response and the one you don't want to hear—no.

I was honored to work as the writer with Vonetta Flowers on her first person story, *Running On Ice* (http://snipurl.com/roivf). Vonetta was the first African American to win a gold medal in the Winter Olympics (2002 women's bobsled). In an interview with her coach, he gave me a terrific quotation from Bob Costas at NBC Sports in his wrap-up of the 2002 Winter Games in Salt Lake. I wondered if I could get a printed endorsement from Costas. From experience, I knew how to give this endorsement its best possible chance.

First, I drafted a possible quote and made it tie in a general way to my book manuscript. My real challenge was to reach Bob Costas. I searched the Internet, but my search was futile. Then I called the news room of NBC in New York City and explained my request and my credentials (I touted my journalism connections). Whoever answered the phone gave me the email address for Costas' manager. I drafted an email of introduction explaining my request for an endorsement—including the possible wording, hit send and waited.

To my surprise, a few hours later I received a brief email from the manager saying, "Terry Whalin, I know that name. We'll get back to you." I thought, *Know my name. Who knows my name?* Within the next day, the manager fulfilled her promise and came back with the revised wording on the endorsement, plus permission to use it. My publisher was thrilled to have such an endorsement to use in the publicity for *Running On Ice*. Here's the endorsement from Bob Costas at NBC Sports:

One of the best stories of the 2002 Winter Olympic Games in Salt Lake came in women's bobsled. Vonetta Flowers and her partner, Jill Bakken, won the Gold Medal. Vonetta thus became the first African American to win a Gold Medal in the Winter Games. In

Running On Ice, Vonetta tells the story behind her achievement. To finish first and be the first, that's Vonetta's singular distinction.

Each individual has to determine at what point to put the energy into endorsements. It might be at the end of the project right before publication—or before you even get a contract.

Why? One reason is the sheer work involved to gather them. Few people want to expend this sort of effort for their books, wondering if the effort is worth it. I've been in publishing long enough to know that some books sell better with endorsements. Book buyers will look at a book in a bookstore or on a conference table and make an instant buying decision. Sometimes they purchase the book because of the endorsement. The endorsements or foreword for the book can also influence the store buyers (the people who make decisions whether to carry your title in their stores or chain of stores).

Consider the audience who will influence the purchase of this book—which names saying positive things about the book will draw the reader to your book. I understand why some authors don't bother with endorsements—because they do take more work and effort. I know from working in the publishing business, however, that endorsements can make the difference as to whether a publisher takes your nonfiction book proposal and offers you a book contract. I recommend that you consider how you can get endorsements for your proposal.

Secret #11

Always Include a SASE

**Always include a self-addressed stamped
envelope for a response, from the publisher.**

IT IS PRESUMPTUOUS TO ASSUME because you invested in
an overnight package that the publisher is going to put postage on
your manuscript and return it to you. A publisher who receives
thousands of unsolicited proposals and manuscripts each year will
not invest in the expense of returning such documents. Instead they
will be discarded. Only if you include return postage for a letter
response or an email address will you be able to receive the rejection or personal feedback from the editor.

Because of the volumes of proposals, publishers are not going to
devote their financial resources to returning those without a SASE.
The cost is too prohibitive and unnecessary. It is the author's responsibility to provide the publisher with an email address or return

postage for their submission. Neglecting this detail is a dead give-away that you are unpublished.

Also don't expect a personal response—even if you met an editor at a writer's conference and used that information in the introductory paragraph of your cover letter. I have taught at many writers' conferences, sometimes almost one a month. I met literally thousands of new people. It's hard to keep all of those details straight. My schedule was fairly typical for an acquisitions editor in the publishing industry.

No editor likes to write rejection letters, yet it comes with the job description. Remember also that the editor isn't running a critique service for your proposal or manuscript when it is rejected. They would like to give a personal response with each rejection, but with the volume of submissions, it simply isn't possible. If you do get a handwritten note or any sort of personal feedback, realize the encouragement and positive nature of this small sign from the editor—and do take it to heart. If they write, "This one isn't right for us, but you should keep trying," then keep trying with a *different* book proposal.

It is ironic to me that year after year at writers' conferences I see the same writer trying to sell the same book proposal to the same editors. I admire persistence, but in some cases persistence is taken to ridiculous lengths. If a publishing house turns down your nonfiction proposal, move on to another publishing house. Some writers work hard on marketing a single nonfiction book proposal or nonfiction manuscript and repeatedly walk with great anxiety each day to their mailbox to see if it is accepted. Instead of this single focus, I suggest you turn your attention to another nonfiction book proposal or a magazine article (something shorter where you can be successful and published).

During my years in publishing, I sent proposals to a variety of publishing houses, either personally or through an agent, and some of these proposal have not sold or contracted. Instead of continuing to push them into the market, I've tucked them into a folder and pressed on to another proposal or idea. From my perspective, the world is not limited to a single idea or a single project. You will have far greater success as a writer with multiple projects in the works, instead of continually focusing on a single proposal. When you mail a stack of proposals to publishers or agents, give yourself a few days of rest, then begin writing another nonfiction book proposal to send out into the market.

During my seven years of running my own freelance business, I commonly had five different books contracted at any given time. This idea made some writers' heads swim, wondering how I kept track of them. I simply staggered the deadlines for the various books, and worked on a new proposal and a current manuscript all the time. It gave me a steady stream of work and income. It also meant that when I completed a manuscript or a proposal, I started on another one. You may work differently, but I encourage you to have multiple ideas and multiple proposals in various stages of completion so you will increase your chances of success and publication.

Understand the importance of including a self-addressed, stamped envelope or an email address for a response. And if you don't want your proposal or manuscript returned, then be sure your cover letter clearly states this information. It's a key secret to your success.

Secret #12

Never Trust the Spellchecker

Don't delegate the spelling in your proposal to a computer.

BOOK PROPOSALS REQUIRE a lot of work and anything you send to a publisher should be completely error and typo-free. Always remember that the ear is less forgiving than the eye. Take the time to read every page of your proposal *aloud*. Hold a pen or pencil as you read, and when you find a mistake or something to adjust, correct it on the spot.

Recently an author sent a manuscript that I read. When I informed her that it had numerous typographical or spelling errors, she instantly became defensive and said she had spellchecked it numerous times. The English language has many similar words which your word processor program will not completely catch. You will have to read and re-read your proposal aloud in order to catch these types of errors.

Here is an example of two sentences that only a person can fix:

The red book was read.

The read book was red.

Each sentence is technically correct, but which one did the author intend to use?

Consider also taking your proposal to a critique group of other writers. (If you want to learn more about this topic, read my detailed article at http://snipurl.com/criti.)

Be careful who you let read your proposal, and always take the feedback of family members with a grain of salt. Ultimately, you are the only person whose opinion on the proposal counts before you send it to a publisher and get their feedback. Some people tend to absorb every positive and negative word from other people. They need to evaluate the comments, take the good ones and discard the poor ones (purely a subjective call on your part).

After receiving this feedback, make sure you've corrected and rewritten every sentence of your proposal and sample chapter to the best of your ability. This type of detailed editorial approach to your proposal will aid in the reception of your materials at the publishing house. Too many proposals and cover letters arrive with missing and misspelled words. Your proposal will rise above the others if you have handled this concern with care and professionalism.

Secret #13

Never Submit Your First Draft

**Your first draft is only the beginning,
not polished enough for sending to a publisher.**

WHEN YOUR PROPOSAL IS completed, lay it aside for several days before you send it. You will then be able to read it with fresh insight and make valuable improvements. Remember the old adage that says, "Haste makes waste." This is particularly true when it comes to writing book proposals. You want to make sure that every single word and sentence of your proposal and sample chapter are excellent. Never rush the process because it will result in less than your best work.

From years of working in magazine production, I've learned one of the most difficult things to find on any publication is something that is completely missing. Yet if something is missing, it will clearly stick out to the reader (in this case, the editor and publishing executives). *Before* you send the proposal is the time to catch any errors.

I've had fearful authors call me and request that I discard their first submission because of some missing element or incorrect element or poor format. You can only imagine the sloppy impression these calls make on your editor. It's not the type of glowing impression an author wants to leave.

I'd encourage you never to forget the relational side of publishing. Often your relationship will be more significant than your printed work with a publisher—especially when it comes to what the editor will remember. Editors will move from publisher to publisher and when this happens, they remember the authors they enjoyed working with on a project at their former publisher. You want to be an author in this particular category. Occasionally editors will brainstorm a particular book they would like to publish and approach an author. When these editors are tossing out names, they will include only those authors who made a professional impression. While this list will not be written anywhere, your editor will recognize excellence and want to take that excellence to a new publisher.

Here are some last minute questions to ask yourself about your proposal and sample chapter:

- Have you hooked the editor with your opening sentence?
- Have you included a solid overview or the "big picture" concept of the book?
- Have you created a catchy title and subtitle, along with some alternatives?
- Is your chapter outline logical and do your chapter summaries address the various points of your book in clear and concise language?
- Have you clearly outlined your vision for the book in terms of length or word count, overall appearance and any special features? Also, have you included the estimated time to deliver the

entire manuscript?

- Have you listed names of well-known experts that you can secure through your personal relationships who will supply endorsements or a foreword?
- Have you detailed your credentials for writing this book in the "About the Author" section and shown without a doubt that you are the best person for this task?
- Have you provided a detailed analysis of the competition for your proposed book and shown how your project is distinct from this competition?
- Have you written a thorough marketing section about the projected audience and how you will join the publisher in a partnership to reach this market?
- Have you highlighted any special marketing and sales opportunities you can bring to the project when it is published? For example, is there a special sale with thousands of books that you can create for the project?
- Have you created a dynamic sample chapter that is compelling and clearly shows your writing style?

There is no right or wrong way to create a nonfiction book proposal. The proposals that sell, however, are the ones in which the author thoroughly presents the concept and includes all of the necessary information. In Appendix B of this book, I include a checklist you can use to prepare nonfiction book proposals.

Secret #14

Maintain a Log of Your Submissions

You need to keep a record of your submissions and follow-up.

AFTER YOU HAVE THE VARIOUS PARTS of the proposal and sample ready, prepare a list of publishers to whom to submit your proposal. Throughout the process of creating a nonfiction book proposal, hopefully you have been focused on the market and a possible list of publishers for your book. Often when I go through this process, I will make a list of different publishers and even rank them as my first choice, second choice, etc. At this point in the process, you want to write your specific list of different publishers. Take a sheet of paper or open a file in your word processor and keep track of the title of the proposal, the names of the publisher and the date you sent it.

Some authors include a self-addressed postcard with their submission on which the editor or editorial assistant can check a box and return it to you. Put the publisher's name in the return address section, then on the reverse side of the postcard write the following:

Dear_____ (write your own name in this blank):

I received your proposal entitled: _____(name of your proposal).

_____

Editor

This postcard will provide you with the reassurance that your proposal arrived safely and is entered into the publisher's system for processing unsolicited manuscripts. It eliminates any need to call or email the editor. There is no need to overnight your proposal or send it through a carrier like FedEx which wastes your money and may cause more negative attention than positive.

Okay. Now your proposal is in that consideration pile. How long do you wait until you contact the editor to check on it? Each situation is different. I've already explained the busy life of an editor with their travel to conferences, frequent meetings and many other responsibilities, so one of the keys for you to answer this question is: How well do you know this particular editor? Do you know him or her personally? If so, how personally? Take a minute and make an honest evaluation of your relationship. Did you meet the editor once or twice at a writers' conference? The level of your relationship will depend on how soon to contact this editor. If you have never met them in person and only corresponded through email or on the phone, then you need to have patience and wait.

I try to be cordial and friendly to everyone, but sometimes writers assume that because I try to promptly answer someone's email or return their phone call, they assume that I'm eager to have an ongoing relationship with them. It's not necessarily true. The key is to look at your relationship honestly; then you will know you should wait rather than annoy the editor.

Agents are your allies at this point in the submission process. As an editor, I regularly receive submissions and talk with various agents who are often former book editors and understand the pressures of an editor much better than the author client. In general, the agent knows when an appropriate amount of time has passed to inquire about a particular manuscript. And they also know when to wait.

For example, last week an agent called me to see how things were going (his first reason for calling), then he got around to his real reason for calling (to see if I received a novel he sent me as fiction acquisitions editor). Yes, I received it but I hadn't read it. This gave him another chance for a verbal pitch about how great this novel will be when I read it. Because of my long-term relationship with this particular agent, he had the "right" to call me and inquire about it.

As an author, you have to recall the old adage, "The squeaky wheel gets greased." Here's the problem: If you never inquire or follow-up on your proposal, you could wait a long time to receive an answer from an editor. Some of my writer friends mention that a particular publisher has had their book proposal for over a year. Whenever I hear that a proposal has been at a publisher for that length of time, there is a high probability the publisher has (a) lost the proposal and will never return it, or (b) will reject the proposal entirely. My experience in publishing says the longer a nonfiction proposal is in circulation, often the less likely the book will be acquired from a traditional publisher. A nonfiction book proposal from a published author with a timely topic is generally purchased in a matter of a few months, rather than many months. The other proposals are held for thorough reading and consideration but even then most of them will be rejected.

Last year, I received an unsolicited call from an author who had published books, but it was a new relationship to me. She explained that she had some devotional books that had gone out of print and wanted to send them for consideration. Our publishing list did include devotional books but we rarely added new titles and they were not on our list of hotly desired topics. While I knew this background when she called, the path of least resistance (or the shortest phone call and interruption) was to encourage her to send me the material. Besides the lack of acquisitions priority for devotional books, I didn't tell this author that sometimes it's harder to get a book reprinted after it's gone out of print than to get it published the first time. Many books go out of print each year because of poor or slacking sales, and you would be surprised at the number of authors who attempt to try and place them with a different publishing house. If I would have explained all these details behind the difficulty of republishing her book, it would have simply lengthened the phone conversation and taken time away from other things I needed to accomplish. I encouraged her to send the material to my attention.

In a few days, her package with the out-of-print books arrived on my desk. I wasn't eager to read the material nor was I quick to return it in light of more pressing priorities. The material was stuck in a pile on my desk. A few weeks later, she called to check on the material and I still had not read it. A few weeks later, I got a third call from this author and immediately I dug out the material and tucked it in an envelope to return it. She pressed for an answer and got the one she didn't want to hear—"No." In the press of returning hundreds of manuscripts, I did not take the time to scribble a note of reason on my rejection letter which I sent her for several reasons— including the annoying repeat phone calls.

I encourage you to keep track of your submissions and follow-up, but do so gently and appropriately. If you push the editor, you will get the answer of least resistance and the one you don't want to hear.

Secret #15

Build Editor Relationships

**Publishing is a relational business.
It is important to build and maintain those relationships.**

AN OLD SAYING is applicable to this secret: "It's not *what* you know but *who* you know." This adage isn't totally true with book proposals and book publishing. You do need to know *what* to send to a publisher to meet their expectations, which I encourage through the bulk of this book. Once you understand and write the format for the proposal, the next key ingredient is a relationship with an editor within a publishing house.

You may wonder, Where do I meet these editors? Plan on attending one or two writers' conference a year. Hundreds of them are held annually around the world (see http://snipurl.com/confer). Part of the conference agenda is to help writers realize that editors are regular people who love words and books and magazines. At these conferences, you can eat meals together, discuss books at a coffee break and begin to form a casual relationship. It's also an opportunity to exchange business cards and talk about the specifics of what the editor is looking to acquire for their publishing house.

Almost everyone at these conferences attends for the main purpose of selling the editor a manuscript, proposal or magazine article. The aim of new writers, however, should be to gather information about the publishing business, rather than to sell an article or book project. The goals for these writers take a dramatic shift during the teaching sessions and they return home with renewed determination to learn the business and reshape their idea. Other writers come to a particular conference year after year and they intentionally target a particular group of editors for their work. These prepared writers study the market and the particular publishers before the conference and target ideas that are appropriate for that publisher or editor.

The editors are eager to talk with these prepared professionals because they have done their homework and are the people most likely to have something the editor needs and wants.

Don't be like some of the people who attend these conferences. This particular brand of writer doesn't want to interact with the editors; rather, they take the hit-and-run approach. During a conference where I was representing a publishing house, I was engaged in a conversation with a writer during a coffee break when another writer interrupted us. He was roaming through the crowd reading name badges (editors usually wear a different color ID at these conferences). When he found one of his targets, he thrust a manuscript into their hands. He looked at my name tag and, knowing that our house took children's material, he reached into his briefcase, pulled out a bound copy of a manuscript and almost threw it into my hands. "You need this manuscript," he said. "I read it in the elementary schools and the kids loved it."

I graciously thanked the writer for his manuscript, tucked it into my bag and continued my previous conversation. At a glance, I could tell that the manuscript title didn't merit any attention. The writer had included rudimentary and ugly drawings throughout and his format marked him as a beginner. This writer definitely made an impression, but rudeness, like politeness, is memorable. In my role as an editor I didn't have a "blacklist" per se, but in my mind, I knew that if I acquired some writers' books, these authors were not going to be good representatives of their books or the publisher. It's important during your face-to-face interaction with an editor to make sure your impression is positive and lasting.

Many times through attending conferences, I've met a new editor, hit it off personally, then collected a book contract or a magazine assignment—sometimes even several contracts or assignments. The roots of that relationship began through talking casually during a conference setting.

My first published book was born as a concept during a writers' conference. A particular children's editor knew that I wrote and edited magazine articles for a missionary publication. Because I had gotten to know this editor, she also knew that I wrote for a variety of magazines and was beginning to establish a reputation as a writer who could deliver the right idea for the right assignment.

Walking together after a meal, this editor stopped me and said, "Terry, our mission statement as a company says that we teach children about missions. Yet of the many books we publish, we don't have a single book that tells children about missions. Do you have some children's book ideas in this area?" Before I tell you my response, let me point out that this editor had a specific need for a specific type of book. Rather than sit back and wait for this book to "magically" appear in her group of manuscripts, she proactively approached someone about the idea. As an acquisitions editor, I am constantly meeting new people and taking the same steps. Often I will proactively approach an author that I know is working in a particular topic area, rather than sit passively and wait for the manuscript to come to me.

I thought about the editor's question for a moment before I offered some book ideas. At the time I was reading and reviewing children's books for a number of publications. I understood and knew what was being done in this area (another key to finding a good idea is to understand the competition). I had read a series of books from Lion by Steve Lawhead called Howard books: *Howard Had A Hot Air Balloon*, *Howard Had A Space Ship*, etc. These books tapped into the child's imagination by using a cartoon character to represent Howard, then combining the character with real pictures from a balloon or space.

"What if we used a cartoon character to represent the child reading the book and combined it with real pictures to show them that they can go anywhere for Jesus?" I suggested.

We talked a bit more and she said, "That's a good idea. Write that up and send it to me."

Did you catch that sentence? She liked my idea and wanted to see it written on paper after the conference. It was an open invitation to send in my work and have it fill an editor's need. As a magazine editor and an acquisitions editor for the book division, I've been shocked at how many times no one picks up on this invitation and encouragement to submit specific material. The editor's world is extremely busy and if you get this type of encouragement, pick up on it and follow through.

In the case of this book editor's invitation, I followed up then submitted my manuscript for her consideration. My first version wasn't exactly on target but over a few months, I received specific feedback about my submission which I revised accordingly, and resubmitted it. About four or five months later, I attended a convention and met with the editor and she presented my first book contract. It wasn't a huge advance or the most generous royalty terms, but this little children's story launched my book writing career.

Just remember the key to this secret is building that relationship with the editor. Understand that editors are real people with families and they experience the same daily struggles you're going through. Care enough to express appreciation and build these relationships. Many of my fellow writers wonder how it happens that I've been involved in so many book writing projects. It's not lightning or rocket science. It's simply that I know many people and I'm always building and maintaining my editor relationships. I keep detailed track of information about people such as their birthdays and anniversaries, the names of their spouses and children. Then right before I talk with them, I review the information so I have it fresh in my mind before I talk with them. When I ask a family question to an editor, it acknowledges that they are a "real" person with a life and concerns. This specific question builds my relationship with this particular editor.

The editors in publishing move around and change companies, but they take their relationships with them. It's an important secret to maintain and build new relationships with editors. They are your friends and they hold the keys to your book publishing contracts.

Secret #16

Delete Any Hype

**Remove any hype or promise from your proposal
that you cannot deliver.**

WE'RE ALMOST DONE with the details of the proposal. Take
the time to go through it one more time and look at every detail with
an evaluative eye. Have you over-promised anywhere in the proposal?
If so, it will stick out in a glaring fashion to the acquisitions editor,
as well as the members of the publication board.

When I received a proposal that promised an endorsement from
best-selling author Beth Moore, I scoffed, "Right." Then I picked up
the phone and asked the author about it. While this author had never published a book, she was an active speaker and it turned out she
had a personal relationship with Beth Moore and access to get the
endorsement. My skepticism turned into genuine encouragement for
this author's proposal.

From the massive amounts of submissions and the overall incomplete and poor quality, the editors become a bit jaded at some lines in proposals. Often proposals will promise an endorsement from some well-known religious leader such as Charles Swindoll or Max Lucado or Chuck Colson. I've worked with many of these leaders on different projects over the years and have a personal relationship with them—yet I would be hard pressed to get an endorsement or foreword for a book from them. It would be hype if I promised it in one of my nonfiction book proposals. I know that the majority of these prominent leaders lead nonprofit organizations governed by a board of directors. In most cases, this board has a blanket policy prohibiting these leaders from endorsing books or lending their names to various projects. While often asked for such endorsements, this prohibition from the board gives the celebrity a polite and impersonal way to decline. Unless you have a long-term friendship or unusual relationship with these people, don't promise or even mention you will attempt to get their endorsement. Such a promise stands to be more hype than reality—and such hype will call the validity of the rest of your nonfiction book proposal into question.

It is acceptable, however, to promise to pursue endorsements to the highest level of your ability and provide a willingness to work with the publisher to brainstorm endorsement possibilities and how to secure them. This gentle and generic expression shows you are in touch with the necessity of endorsements and your availability to use whatever moxie and connections you have to promote the book.

Secret #17

Use a Well-Crafted Proposal to Snag an Agent

An excellent, well-crafted proposal might be your first step to getting an agent.

WHEN YOU BEGIN TO LOOK FOR publishing houses to send your manuscript, you will note that many of these houses have an imaginary sign posted that proclaims, "Not interested. No matter what manuscript or proposal you are planning to send."The sign may not be this blunt but they use terms like "only reviewing agented proposals" or "no longer accepting unsolicited proposals." Sometimes the publisher will refer you to a service such as The Writer's Edge or The First Edition, ECPA Manuscript Service. You can pursue these services if you want and they are a possibility. Or you can use your polished nonfiction book proposal as a means to catch the attention of a literary agent.

Agents can open doors for your book that you may not be able to open on your own. A good one can provide valuable insight and feedback about your proposal before he sends it to various publishing houses. Also the good agents know about publishing needs that you as a writer will be hard pressed to find out. They are constantly talking with editors from different publishing houses, learning about needs and brainstorming how they can fill those needs with the clients that they represent. It's well worth their 15 percent fee from your overall earnings. I would not use any agent who charges a reading fee, however. It's not normal. If you want to know more about where to look for an agent and what types of questions to ask, read Victoria Strauss's excellent article, "The Safest Way to Search for An Agent" at http://snipurl.com/safest.

One way to get an agent is to ask for referrals from other writers who have agents. To make your selection easier, ask the agent the questions suggested on the Association of Author Representatives (AAR) website (http://snipurl.com/aarfaq). Not every good agent is a member of AAR, but the membership requirements of the association make an AAR member a worthy agent to consider.

Agents can also help in shaping your proposal as illustrated in the excellent book by Noah Lukeman, *The First Five Pages, A Writer's Guide to Staying Out of the Rejection Pile* (http://snipurl.com/Firstfive). Lukeman is a New York City literary agent. In the opening pages, he writes,

> Over the last few years, I've read thousands of manuscripts, all, unbelievably, with the exact same type of mistakes. From Texas to Oklahoma to California to England to Turkey to Japan, writers are doing the exact same things wrong. While evaluating more than ten thousand manuscripts in the last few years, I was able to group these mistakes into categories, and eventually, I was able to set forth definite criteria, an agenda for rejecting manuscripts...Agents and editors don't read manuscripts to enjoy them; they read solely with the goal of getting through the pile, solely with an eye to dis-

miss a manuscript—and believe me, they'll look for any reason they can, down to the last letter.

Another good tool for anyone looking for an agent is an out-of-print book, *Literary Agents: A Writer's Introduction* by John F. Baker (MacMillan USA, 1999). http://snipurl.com/literary. Baker has written for *Publisher's Weekly* for many years and in this book, he profiles a series of literary agents in the business. You will learn a great deal about agents through reading this excellent book, and it may give you some ideas about what agent to approach with your project. While the good agents usually have a full list of clients, they are always looking for a great idea that meets their interests and markets. You may find your match through a careful reading of Baker's book.

Agents, like editors, are looking for projects they can be enthusiastic about, and they like to convey that enthusiasm to their publishing contacts. If you have crafted an excellent nonfiction proposal and followed the other "secrets" in this book, then you have positioned yourself for an agent to represent your project to some major and minor publishing houses.

Perhaps, however, you are worried about the economics and giving up 15 percent of your earnings. From my experience, it's better to have something than nothing. If you never place your own proposals with a publisher, what have you managed to accomplish through this process? On the other hand, what if your proposal interests an agent and he turns around and places your book with a publisher that only takes projects submitted through literary agents (and there are many of these publishers in today's market) and gets a $8,000 advance for you? This is $8,000 you didn't have before he came into your life. Even if it's $5,000, from my perspective that would still be worth it. The agent is someone who can review your contract, encourage you when you need it and run interference with your editor or publisher, if needed.

Agents need excellent projects (and clients) for their own work needs. If you can find that agent relationship, it may begin with your hard work on a nonfiction book proposal. Finding a good agent takes as much work as finding a good publisher. While many editors move around from publisher to publisher, many authors stay with the same agent for years. This agent becomes a trusted friend, encourager and a source of work and inside publishing information. Using a well-crafted nonfiction book proposal to snag a well-connected literary agent is a valuable "secret" for every writer.

Secret #18

Proposal Writing Takes Lots of Work

Don't kid yourself that the process of proposal writing is simple. It takes lots of work that many people don't want to do—so they fail. Don't fail.

I'VE TAUGHT SOME OF THE MATERIAL in this book a number of times at writers' conferences. After several hours of teaching and the details involved in putting together a well-done nonfiction book proposal, I can see the dismay on the faces of the individuals in my session. They are thinking, "Hey, this is going to be a lot of work!"

And they're exactly right. To write an excellent book proposal *is* a great deal of work and effort. It's not a get rich quick scheme or a quick fix. Advertising tries to convince us that we need a magic bullet that will bring us success. It doesn't exist. Instead, you need to complete the work, step-by-step. If you create a nonfiction proposal and sample which is complete, then you have given the publisher exactly what they need to make a decision. Also you have separated your work from the multitude of other projects that pour into a publishing house. You have proven that you have what it takes to write a quality book project.

Because we live in a world looking for shortcuts and the easy way out, you must be aware that success comes by taking the narrow path. If you do the work and complete everything needed for the proposal, you will succeed when others fail. It's a critical secret to creating a book proposal that sells. You must do the work.

Secret #19

Submit Your Proposal Simultaneously

Develop a solid list of places to submit your proposal and submit your proposal *simultaneously*.

EARLIER IN THIS BOOK, I've explained about the busy life of an editor and how difficult it is for them to find the time to read your proposal. It's not uncommon to wait several months to receive a response from a publishing house. One literary agent told me that he received a rejection from a well-known publisher over a year after a competitive publishing house had released the book. This agent just shook his head at the length of time it took to receive that rejection. His story points out the unpredictable nature of rejection—even for a well-known agent. Agents supposedly receive faster service from acquisitions editors because their submissions are read with greater priority than unsolicited, unagented submissions. I say "supposedly" because I know as an editor I read some agent's submissions quicker than others. It depends on my relationship with a particular agent and my knowledge about whether his material usually meets my editorial needs—among other factors.

My key point from this story is that you need to submit your manuscript *simultaneously*—that is, to more than one publishing house or one agent at a time, and make sure you note this fact in your cover letter. These words tell the editor that other editors and publishers also will be reading this proposal—possibly at the same time. If you receive a contract on a simultaneous submission and decide to sign with this particular publisher, then you need to notify the other places you sent the proposal and ask them to remove this project from consideration.

I've mentioned previously the difficult consensus building process that an acquisitions editor has to use so a writer receives a publishing contract. Look at this situation from the editor's viewpoint. They have worked inside their publishing house for weeks to get everyone's agreement and be able to make an offer. Imagine their consternation if they learn that another publisher has beat them to the punch and they didn't know about it. If the writer hasn't been in close communication with this editor, the editor will remember his name (in a negative sense) for a long time. Once again, good communication with the publishing houses permits you to send out your proposal simultaneously without any possible penalty.

The other caveat about simultaneous submission is not to accept two contracts from two different publishers. Books are expensive to produce. If publisher A begins to produce the book at the same time publisher B begins to produce the book, you will cause a large uproar when the double contract is discovered and be banned from this particular area of publishing. I'm not exaggerating when I use the word "banned." Admittedly this type of situation would be rare but it is possible. You as the author control the contracts you ultimately sign and you can prevent this possibility from occurring.

Because of the length of time it takes to make a decision, publishers aren't concerned when they see the words "simultaneous submission" on a proposal. The words will clue the editor to be in careful communication with the author throughout the process. As an acquisitions editor, I would call an author and tell them when I was going to present their work to the publishing board and keep them informed as the project progressed through the process toward a contract. Good communications on the part of the editor and the writer will make for a successful book project.

Okay, now we have established the importance of you submitting your work simultaneously. You can submit simultaneously to a number of literary agents with the same caveat—maintain good communication with them. If you are going to pursue the agent route, however, it is advisable *not* to send out your proposal to various publishers at the same time. If you have extensively marketed a particular book proposal to publishers, then your work will make it less attractive for a literary agent to represent to some of the same publishers. Doesn't this make sense? Agents are in the business to sell great proposals to publishers. You don't want to interfere in this process.

My recommendation is to prepare a list of ten to fifteen publishers to whom you can submit your completed nonfiction book proposal. Because of your work on the competition for your proposal or your knowledge of the book-publishing world, who would you like to publish your book?

With this list in hand, begin with those publishers where you know an editor—one you may have met at a writers' conference or one with whom you have a personal connection. If you don't have such a connection, there are several ways you can establish one:

• Look at some books that record the editor's name and note that connection in your cover letter.
• Attend a writers' conference once or twice a year. (For more information on conferences, check out http://snipurl.com/conferences

• Like the editor, see which literary agents are thanked in similar books. It can give you a clue about which one to approach with your proposal.

Possibly you are so new to the writing world that you don't have any personal connection to publishing houses. Don't worry about it. You can still send out your proposal. One of the consistent failures of many new writers is a lack of persistence and perseverance in their marketing efforts. I recall one writer who submitted his proposal a couple of times, received rejection notices, put the proposal into a file and never marketed it again. Small wonder this writer never found a publisher who would take his nonfiction book proposal. He lacked enough persistence to get it into the market for consideration.

One of the best market guides published each year is the *Writer's Market* from Writer's Digest Books. Purchase the current edition because a great deal of information changes each year. Or if you don't want to purchase the guide, almost every public library in the nation maintains this book in their reference section. You may not be able to check it out, but you can photocopy or write down the information you need at the library.

Another excellent resource is *Jeff Herman's Guide to Book Publishers, Editors and Literary Agents 2004: Who They Are! What They Want! and How to Win Them Over!* (Writer's Guide to Book Editors, Publishers, and Literary Agents) by Jeff Herman, a literary agent. Or if you are writing Christian material, make sure you get Sally E. Stuart's *Christian Writer's Market Guide* which is absolutely the best product in this area.

One key to remember is to use the *latest* market guides. Editors move from company to company and the information in these guides changes with each edition. The name of a former editor on your proposal marks you as someone who hasn't done their homework. It's worth a quick phone call to an editorial assistant to double check the name on your cover letter and envelope.

Why put so much energy and effort into making sure you have the right editor's name? Because another little known fact of publishing is that many editors do not have assistants or secretaries to open, sort and process their mail. If the envelope is addressed to this editor, then he will be the person to open the package and read your cover letter and proposal. Earlier in this book, I've explained how slow some editors are to open their email, but it should be some encouragement that the person that you want to read your nonfiction book proposal will actually be the person opening the package. This fact should motivate you to give your proposal the most professional appearance possible and not send anything out of the ordinary. It is your writing and proposal that will have to sell the editor and eventually others inside the publishing house.

In addition to marketing guides, you can also use the publisher's Internet websites to gather information for submission. Be aware of how often a particular website is updated. Does it contain their latest publishing releases? Do the guidelines look like they have been updated recently? I do a lot of reading and study in the publishing arena and I've noticed some publishers are more active in updating their website material than others. Just because you received the information on a website doesn't mean the information is current. It's your responsibility as the writer to double check such information.

Now you've developed a list of publishers where you plan to simultaneously submit your nonfiction book proposal. I suggest you send your proposals to five different publishers at the same time, and make sure you keep excellent records of your submissions. This submission system doesn't have to be complicated. When I started writing and submitting to magazines and book publishers, I used a simple composition notebook that cost less than $3. You can use the same system. Here's how it works:

Take the first few pages of the notebook and call it "Table of

Contents."

1. For every new article or book proposal create a new page in your notebook. Index that page with your table of contents.

2. On the specific page for a nonfiction proposal called "Catch the Tiger By the Tail, Keys for Busy Parents," keep a running list of the places you are sending your proposal. Jot down the first publisher, the date you sent your submission and note their response. If you send a follow-up postcard or email, note the date of that correspondence. At a glance you can see what is happening with a particular project. Then make sure you proactively check on it, but don't be a nuisance to the editor. Remember the easiest answer for an editor to give is the answer you don't want to hear—"No."

3. Flip to the back of your composition notebook and count about ten pages from the back. You are going to create another section called "Submissions."

4. On your "Submissions" page, put the date in the far left hand side, then draw a straight line down the page. Beside the date (after where you drew the line), write the name of the proposal or article.

5. Now draw another line on the other side of the name of the proposal or article. In this spot, record the response—Yes or No. At a glance to your submission page, you can see which publishers have not responded and note your need to follow-up with a quick email or a postcard or a short phone call (rare).

For many years of my writing career, I used the composition notebook system to track my submissions. It's thorough, cost-effective and simple—yet allows you to have a professional way of monitoring the progress or lack of progress with your submission process and keep excellent records in a compact location.

Secret #20

Get More Proposals Out the Door

Develop patience while waiting for a response—but don't pace in front of your mailbox. Instead get more ideas and proposals out the door.

FOR YEARS, I'VE BEEN INVOLVED IN the writing community—as a writer and also as an editor. From talking with writers at conferences, I know that they often like to choose an easy target for complaining—editors and publishers. The editor takes too long to respond or they lose the manuscript or the manuscript is returned dog-eared with coffee spills and a rejection letter.

In an earlier portion of this book, I explained that an editor has much more to do than read your proposal or idea—no matter how brilliant or excellent or perfect for that publisher. From my perspective, these writers who complain are simply trying to point the finger away from themselves and their own lack of skill.

I also meet with writers at conferences on an individual basis where I listen to their ideas. Whenever I realize it's unlikely that their idea will fly in *any* publishing house, I try and say something gracious and let them down gently. The next time, I return to this same conference and this same writer meets with me about the same idea. Or maybe they have modified it ever so slightly. Possibly last time, the idea was a Christian living book and now it has been changed into a series of devotions—but it is basically the same unworkable concept from the year before.

Like many professional writers, I have a series of folders in my files of book proposals that I never sold. Despite my many book sales, I have not sold every idea or every concept. Rejection continues to be a part of my writing life. I've learned to accept that some of these ideas just haven't found the right home or maybe I haven't shaped them in the right way—yet—or possibly never.

When I hear writers complaining about the slow response from editors, I tend to take a different course of action—and one that I recommend you take as well. Instead of pacing back and forth to my mailbox or email box, I turn and begin more projects. For example, at the moment, my writing schedule isn't completely full. I'd like to have a few more book contracts in the works. While some editor may call me tomorrow and fill my schedule, it's like getting struck by lightning—I'm not counting on it.

Instead, I am proactively working every day to create new projects and new opportunities. In the early days of television, I watched the Ed Sullivan Show. One of his frequent guests was a man who came out with a number of long sticks and china dinner plates. He would begin with one spinning plate and, in a matter of minutes, this performer had the entire stage covered with sticks and spinning plates. If you need to have more writing work, what are you actively doing to fill your writing schedule? How can you spin some additional plates?

After you complete your particular nonfiction book proposal

using the secrets in this book, start another nonfiction book proposal and get this second idea into the marketplace. Or write something shorter like a magazine article, then write some query letters, snag an assignment and begin the article. The prolific and productive writers that I know are all working on multiple projects.

Every writer needs to learn patience, and the best way I've been able to handle patience is to plunge into a new endeavor. I recommend you take the same course of action and create more writing projects. It will improve your possibilities for success, consistent and continued work.

Secret #21

Always Take the
Attitude of a Learner

Never "arrive" in your thinking and craft of writing. Continually work at building a "body of work."

YOU MAY WONDER WHAT this final secret has to do with writing a book proposal that sells. The answer is that your attitude will creep into your proposal, the words that you select and your impromptu conversation with the editor or the publicist.

I want you to take this attitude throughout your writing experience—whether you create these proposals multiple times or only once. I never take for granted the conferences I teach at, recalling my own insecure feelings when I attended my first conference about 20 years ago. It's pretty easy to be full of yourself and your own experience at these conferences. People pay large sums of money to sit and listen to your lectures throughout the week. Many conferences require the faculty to "host" a table with your name on it and the various attendees arrive early to make sure they get a close seat at your table.

At these conferences, everyone wants to talk with the editors because they are the ones with the power to purchase their manu-scripts and give them their beginning in publishing. (Remember this is their perspective—not necessarily true because of all the things I've said earlier about how the acquisitions editor has to con-vince many people to contract your book; the same in the magazine world). Editors are elevated at these conferences—and it can go to their head if they believe their own press (something you should nev-er do).

When I taught at one of the largest and oldest writers' conferences in the nation, I stopped and listened to a new writer pitch her idea, then I went off to another conference activity. I received this email from another author about the reaction from the new writer. She begins with my interaction with the attendee:

I watched a young girl talk with you right after lunch. You bent over to hear and listened. (I knew you were on your way some-where...but you stopped.) And then you smiled and I saw you walk away. But while she talked...you focused in. (OK...I'm nosey and a watcher.)

What you DON'T know is the girl came over to me and said, "Did you see, he talked with me and he even listened!"

I have no idea who she was... I know it was her first time at the conference and she mumbled, "He actually listened to me. No one else has."

I practically grabbed her arm. You taught me right there...slow down and remember how it feels when these "big guys" talk the first time! (This is only my third time.) As we sat together, I lis-tened to her excitement about just talking to you. When she was finished, she went to call her mom and tell her she just talked with *one of the editors.* You had no idea how you put the faith back into her to trust God in leading her to write. And you taught me a big lesson too.

While I'm grateful for this sort of feedback from my teaching, I never want to assume that I'm one of the "big guys" or above learning anything from anyone else about how to do better at my craft or writing. It's a conscious choice that I've made with my writing and work and a key secret that you can carry into your writing.

In the early days of my writing career, I was an editor and charged to supervise an older writer who wrote books for this particular organization. To this writer's chagrin, I had to sign all of his financial receipts so he could get reimbursed. One day when he was in my office, I inquired if he ever attended a writers' conference. He straightened up a bit at the question and responded, "Yes, I attend a conference when they ask me to teach."

He didn't answer my question in the expected way but did give the information that I requested. This writer was beyond attending conferences or meetings to simply learn from the experience. Instead, he attended only when invited to teach. This author had grown to believe his press and loved basking in the attention of being the "expert." Unfortunately, this attitude crept into his writing and almost every other way he was involved in the publishing world. In my opinion, this held him back from becoming better at his craft.

At a different conference, I was surprised to find a best-selling novelist in the crowd of registrants. She is a much sought after keynote speaker at these types of events—and she was simply sitting in the audience. This author had sold more books than anyone on the faculty that particular year. When I stopped her and asked about it, she said she decided to register with her daughter-in-law and take the children's writing continuing class. She was a novelist and had never written a children's book and wanted to learn from the instructor. This humble action made another impression on me that has lasted to this day. Never be content with your particular area of expertise because there is always more to learn or a new area to conquer.

Years ago a literary agent and I were riding together in a van to begin another writers' conference. We were getting acquainted and talking about the business of publishing. He gave me a new term that I'd never heard before—"body of work." I pass this secret along to you in this section. A "body of work" is the sum total of your publishing efforts and it may happen in a few years or many years. I'd encourage you to keep this term in mind and continually work at building a "body of work."

Many people are amazed that in about ten years, I wrote more than 50 nonfiction books. Also I've written for many more than 50 magazines. I continue to write for two new publications. I've found it simpler not to count specifically and to keep my biography saying "written for more than 50 magazines." I didn't wake up one day and suddenly have written this volume of material. Every day I work at building a body of work. In the early days, I didn't have many publishing credits or books to show for this body but I persevered and have consistently written. I'll be the first to confess that I don't believe all of my work is outstanding. Many other writers are more brilliant in their phraseology or syntax and the way they construct images. I've continued to write books in spite of any internal insecurity. I'm committed to growing in my craft and learning how to be a better writer. It's why I continue to read how-to books about writing and different aspects of the craft—despite my publishing track record.

My experience doesn't have to be unique. You can take the attitude of a learner and continually grow in your abilities in the publishing world. It may take you years to craft a nonfiction book proposal that sells or you may accomplish it in a relatively short amount of time. The key is getting up every day and doing your best. I have great expectations about what you can accomplish if you follow these 21 secrets. In reality, these are not secrets but hard-earned lessons about the publishing business. If you follow these suggestions, your proposal will shine and be distinguished from the many others on the editor's desk. It might give you just the right measure of attention to land a book contract.

Sample Book Proposal That Sold for a Six-Figure Advance

Background:

I have a number of books on my shelf about how to write a book proposal. Something that I've never seen is an actual proposal that has sold for a six-figure advance. I've had the opportunity to write two of these types of proposals and I include one of them in this book as an example for you. Note that this proposal did not include a sample chapter to garner this type of attention. It was written in the height of the Promise Keeper movement, when Promise Keepers was the fastest growing men's movement in America and receiving a great deal of media attention.

Book Proposal

THE SEVEN PROMISES

A Spiritual Guide For Men In Today's World

by Bishop Phillip H. Porter, Jr.,

Chairman for the Board of Directors for Promise Keepers

with W. Terry Whalin

Foreword by Bill McCartney, Founder of Promise Keepers

Overview

Most men can count on one hand the other men in their lives with who they can be themselves. Traditionally, women have been anointed the emotional sex, while men have been conditioned to be islands, isolated emotionally from other men. But the winds of change are blowing in this country. Men are looking for ways to reach out, to share their inner spirit with other men.

In fact, men have been seeking this spiritual connection for a long time. In 1990, Robert Bly saw the need for his book, *IRON JOHN*, which helped men overcome the stereotypes of our popular culture. It hit the *New York Times* bestseller list with a vengeance and stayed there for 62 weeks, with 10 weeks at #1. That same year, a college football coach named Bill McCartney and his pastor recognized the emerging climate of change and dreamed about doing something for men. Soon after, they founded "Promise Keepers."

It started small, but as we have all read, it has blossomed quickly. "Promise Keepers" is the fastest growing men's movement in the country. In 1995, the 16 massive national rallies had a combined attendance of 720,000 men. During 1996, "Promise Keepers" projects is reaching 1.5 million men with 23 rallies. These rallies will be held in America's stadiums: New York's Shea Stadium, Chicago's Soldier Field, the Los Angeles Coliseum, the Seattle Kingdome, the Minneapolis Metrodome, Washington's RFK Stadium and Denver's Mile High Stadium. Despite a capacity of 40-60,000 men, many of the upcoming summer events are already sold out. It has been covered closely by all major media including news magazines like *Time*, *Newsweek* and *U.S. News and World Report*, ABC News and numerous pages on the World Wide Web, both official and unofficial. In a word, "Promise Keepers" is nothing less than a phenomenon.

But what is it? Essentially, "Promise Keepers" is a Christ-centered ministry dedicated to uniting men through vital relationships to become godly influences in their world. The values of the organization are captured in seven promises. These "promises" are not a new list of commandments. Rather they set a standard for what it means to be a godly man in today's world. A godly man lives his life with a fresh standard that includes honesty, integrity, and commitment—biblical values which men need to re-visit.

The objective of a "Promise Keeper" is rooted in a basic belief about God. God keeps his covenants and promises to his people. Because God is faithful in his promises, the promises are based on the Bible. Numbers 23:19 says, "God is not a man that he should lie or the son of man that he should repent. Has he said and will he not do it? Has he spoken and will he not fulfill it?"

THE SEVEN PROMISES will serve as the backbone of the book through which Dr. Phillip H. Porter, Jr. will weave his own personal experiences and interpret the promises in ways that all men can understand. Each promise is designed to target a key need and concern for men. The promise is the spiritual solution to an every day problem. As we have already discussed, men have complained about a spiritual emptiness. They want to fill this vacuum. The answer is in the first promise: "Honor Jesus Christ through worship, prayer and obedience to God's Word through the power of the Holy Spirit." Here are the other promises.

The Man's Need: A relationship with other men
Promise Two: Pursue Vital Relationships with A Few Men

The Man's Need: To find truth in a world where deception is commonplace

Promise Three: Practice Spiritual, Moral, Ethical and Sexual Purity

The Man's Need: Preservation of his family amidst skyrocketing divorce

Promise Four: Build a Strong Marriage and Families through love, protection and biblical values

The Man's Need: Somewhere to Grow Stronger Spiritually.

Promise Five: Support the local Church and Honor the Clergy

The Man's Need: To end the tension of race and denominations.

Promise Six: Reach Beyond Racial and Denominational Barriers and Demonstrate the Power of Biblical Unity.

The Man's Need: To influence the world and love his neighbor as himself

Promise Seven: Influence the World and Obey the Great Commission

For the last three years, Bishop Porter has been chairman of the board of directors of "Promise Keepers." Recently re-elected for another year, Bishop Porter is an extremely close colleague and friend of Bill McCartney and is a key person in the movement's future. Last month, 50,000 clergy attended a three day "Promise Keeper" rally in the Atlanta Georgia Dome—an unprecedented nondenominational rally for such a specialized profession. Bishop Porter was one of the keynote speakers. Porter will speak at nine of the "Promise Keeper" rallies around the U.S. in 1996. His book, *The Seven Promises*, will be the first ABA book to be written by a senior "Promise Keeper."

"Promise Keepers" is very determined to break down the walls of racial disharmony, and as an African-American, Bishop Porter believes that "Promise Keepers" represents an alternative for his own community to Farrakhan's Nation of Islam. Farrakhan's Million Man March captured immense media coverage last fall, but it was exclusive to black men. Yes, "Promise Keepers" is a movement for men but it takes a completely opposite stance on the issue of race. The sixth promise of a "Promise Keeper" exhibits this commitment: "A Promise Keeper is committed to reach beyond any racial and denominational barriers to demonstrate the power of biblical unity." For over forty years, Bishop Porter has played a significant role in the concept of racial reconciliation. For example, he integrated an all-white university in Oklahoma in 1955. He will discuss this experience in depth in the book.

During 1997, "Promise Keepers" plans their own million man rally in Washington, D.C. Originally planned for 1996, the "Promise Keepers" intentionally delayed their rally until 1997 because they didn't want it to have a political media spin during an election year. Instead the "Promise Keeper" rally will gather men from all races to show the general public they are committed to stand for their promises—with integrity, honesty and commitment. Because of the moral, spiritual, ethical and sexual decline in America, the "Promise Keepers" sense the need to stand firm for their promises and on that occasion will pray for the nation.

There are some misperceptions that "Promise Keepers" is an upper class, white organization. The founder, Bill McCartney, former football coach of the University of Colorado Buffaloes, is indeed white. But the "Promise Keepers" is racially diverse. During the 1996 rallies, half of the speakers will be minorities. The "Promise Keeper" board of directors includes African Americans, Latin Americans and Native Americans.

Over the last couple of years, there has been an explosion of spiritually-based books which have found their way to bestseller lists.

Novels like *The Celestine Prophecy*, Buddhist books by famous "masters," new age self-help books have all experienced a tremendous upsurge among book buyers, and the time is right for a more Christian-oriented book to hit this eager audience. This Christian spirituality is captured in the pages of *The Seven Promises*.

Chapter Summaries:

Chapter 1
Why Seven Promises?
This chapter explains the basis for the seven values of a "Promise Keeper." Beyond information, the chapter will captivate the reader and draw him into these spiritual topics from Porter's personal experiences. Growing up in a small town in Oklahoma, Porter experienced firsthand the segregated lifestyle of the 1940s and 1950s. He integrated Phillips University, an all-white Disciples of Christ school, and graduated in 1959 with a degree in social work. For his first job out of college, Porter secured a job in Walsenburg, Colorado. A letter in his pocket confirmed the position. When he arrived at the social work office, they said, "The job has been filled," then tore his letter into small pieces. He was the wrong race for that position. Instead of turning bitter, Porter had a life centered on spiritual matters. He knew that God would open up something else. Over thirty years later, Porter started his most prominent position—chairman of the board of "Promise Keepers." More than words, Porter has "walked through his talk." His words and experiences will strike a chord in the heart of every reader.

Chapter 2
Promise One: Honor Jesus Christ
Porter's world as a small child in the 1940s and 1950s was strict segregation—schools, theaters, drinking fountains, restaurants and restrooms. But something different happened on Sunday evening,

in the walls of his church building. African Americans, whites, Hispanics, and Native Americans sat side by side in worship. Racial integration wasn't impossible, thought Porter. The easing of any tension begins with a desire to honor Jesus Christ through worship, prayer and obedience of the truth in the Bible.

Chapter 3
Promise Two: Pursue Vital Relationships with A Few Men

A small "accountability" group is a core part of the "Promise Keepers." At first, Bishop Porter was skeptical about such a group of men. He didn't know if he could be himself with these white men from various denominations and background, but he gave them a chance. They have been meeting weekly for three years and Bishop Porter feels a spiritual connection to this small group. There have been many other experiences like this in Porter's life.

Chapter 4
Promise Three: Practice Spiritual, Moral, Ethical and Sexual Purity

As a teenager in a small Oklahoma town, Porter watched his grandfather and dad work long hours for small wages. This chapter will recount some of those stories and the way Porter learned a careful balance for his life—the importance of depending on God for justice, yet continuing to strive for proper treatment.

Chapter 5
Promise Four: Build Strong Marriage and Families

Porter has worked for years in the African American community of Denver. He's seen the drug lords and crack houses. Yet his own family of eight children and his marriage remains strong. This chapter will give his personal insight for men about how they too can have strong families and marriages.

Chapter 6
Promise Five: Support the Church and Honor the Clergy
From his earliest memories, Bishop Porter learned about the importance of the church. This chapter will help readers learn from the mistakes and successes of Porter during his many years of working across denominations and races.

Chapter 7
Promise Six: Reach Beyond Racial and Denominational Barriers
From his first day at an all-white school, Porter got a smashed watermelon in his face by a white boy. But it didn't stop his integration of an all-white school. When he was refused his first job because of race, it didn't make him bitter. This chapter will highlight the spiritual lessons Bishop Porter has learned about how to live in unity among the races and denominations.

Chapter 8
Promise Seven: Influence the World and Obey the Great Commission
Beyond the city limits of Denver, Porter is working through Promise Keepers to touch the world. As a young man, God showed him a vision about how his life would mean something to a broad audience. This chapter gives men hope and guidance about how to reach beyond their jobs or world into the broader spectrum of the world.

Chapter 9
Dreams for the Future Become Real
How will the world change if men become spiritually sensitive? From Porter's vantage point, this chapter examines the future for men and paints a clear picture of the changes in society and the family. Dr. Porter concludes with a message of hope and encouragement.

About the Author and Co-Author:

Phillip H. Porter, Jr. is the Chairman of the Board of Directors for "Promise Keepers." Porter speaks to this broad-based audience of men about spirituality. A bishop for Montana with the Church of God in Christ, Dr. Porter is the pastor of a Denver congregation, All Nations Pentecostal Center Church of God in Christ.

W. Terry Whalin is the author of over 40 books and has written for over 40 publications. The former Associate Editor at *Decision* with the Billy Graham Evangelistic Association, Terry is a journalism graduate from Indiana University and a twenty-year member of the Society of Professional Journalists. His books include other biographies of Chuck Colson, John Perkins, and Luis Palau. Terry lives in Colorado Springs, Colorado.

The Competition:

There are no broad market books for men interested in "Promise Keepers"—especially in the general marketplace. There have been several "Promise Keepers" books in the CBA (Christian Booksellers Association), but they are virtually non-existent in major chain stores. Bishop Porter's book would be unique because of his position as the Chairman of the Promise Keeper Board of Directors.

Manuscript Delivery and Length:

The manuscript would be 40,000 to 50,000 words in length and could be written in time for the Christmas season or the spring of 1997—timed perfectly with the massive "Promise Keeper" rally in Washington, D.C.

Promotion:

Bishop Porter travels throughout the U.S. and is in regular demand as a speaker. About 75 percent of his time is spent traveling as the Chairman of the Board for Promise Keepers. He would be available for media interviews and book signings. He is accessible and handles the media well. More than an "American" search for spirituality, this "Promise Keepers" movement among men reaches out across the seas. During the last month, Bishop Porter, a prominent African American, has traveled with "Promise Keepers" to England, South Africa and India. Other countries are asking for help from this fast-growing organization.

In June, Creation House will release Porter's first book, *Let the Walls Fall Down* to the Christian Bookseller market. *Let the Walls Fall Down* centers completely on the topic of prejudice and reconciliation while *The Seven Promises* will be a broader look at the topic. Also *The Seven Promises* is a distinct look at spirituality for men in today's world.

Appendix A

Books for Writing Nonfiction Book Proposals

The success or failure of a book proposal involves many factors, but you will never get an editor or publisher to consider your proposal if it doesn't arrive in the *expected* format. There is no right or wrong way to do a proposal but almost every publisher expects certain elements. You can learn about these elements from the following books:

The Fast-Track Course on How to Write a Nonfiction Book Proposal by Stephen Blake Mettee. Quill Driver Books. 2002. In an easy-to-read style, Mettee introduces the reader to some basics about publishing, then details about proposal query letters and the actual proposal. Samples of the query, book proposal, agency contract and book contract are included along with a nonfiction book proposal checklist. This book is loaded with great information.

The Shortest Distance Between You and a Published Book, 20 Steps to Success by Susan Page. Broadway Books. 1997. More than about book proposals, Susan Page guides readers through decisions whether to self-publish or sell to a publisher. It includes valuable tips about the nonfiction book proposal but is much broader in focus including areas like negotiating a contract, following book production details such as catalogue copy and publicizing your book.

Write The Perfect Book Proposal, 10 That Sold and Why, 2nd Edition by Jeff Herman and Deborah Levine Herman. John Wiley & Sons, Inc. 2001. This book first explains the basic elements of a book proposal, then these New York literary agents walk you through ten different proposals that sold. You learn the rationale behind the information in a proposal and the age-old truth in publishing—that it continues to be highly subjective from publisher to publisher. One publisher loves it and another rejects it. This book will increase your insight into this truth and how to overcome it.

How to Write A Book Proposal by Michael Larsen. Writer's Digest Books. 1990. If you read *Writer's Digest* magazine, then you will recognize this author. Larsen worked for several publishers before he co-founded the oldest literary agency in San Francisco. As a literary agent, Larsen has seen hundreds of proposals and guided many authors to successful publication. This book is short (115 pages), concisely written and loaded with good advice.

Nonfiction Book Proposals Anybody Can Write, How to Get a Contract and Advance Before Writing Your Book by Elizabeth Lyon. Perigee. 2002. In great detail with numerous illustrations, Lyon walks anyone through the process of creating a nonfiction book proposal. As she writes in the opening pages, "Only a small fraction of those who submit manuscripts understand the importance of using a proposal or know how to write one. This book will give you a critically important edge on the competition."

Inside Religious Publishing, A Look Behind the Scenes by Leonard George Goss and Don M. Aycock, editors. Zondervan Publishing House. 1991. In my opinion, every Christian writer should read this book. I understand from Zondervan that it's now out of print but you can easily track it down through the library. It's the most comprehensive look at the religious market. This book is more than about nonfiction book proposals with insight about fiction and other areas of Christian communication. For nonfiction book proposals, the book covers important concepts such as how do editors decide what to publish (Andrew T. LePeau from InterVarsity Press), what do book editors do? (Dean Merrill, former VP of Publications at Focus and now VP with the International Bible Society), or how to prepare a nonfiction book proposal (Mike S. Hyatt, former literary agent and now President of Thomas Nelson. His chapter has been updated and is now Appendix C in this book). Co-author Len Goss is the Editorial Director at Broadman & Holman.

Story Boarding Techniques

LifeMapping by John Trent, Ph.D. Focus on the Family Publishing. 1998. Walt Disney used a technique for creating stories called Story Boarding. You can also use this technique when creating the overall outline for your nonfiction book project. John Trent's book is not a writing book but contains the techniques for story boarding or outlining your book project—yet with a counseling theme. You can apply the brainstorming, creative techniques to book creation.

Appendix B

Nonfiction Book Proposal Checklist

Is Your Idea Saleable?

☐ Know your audience.

☐ Ask yourself why they would want to read your book.

☐ Research several large bookstores to see if anything is already available.

☐ Check a large major library for competitive titles.

☐ Examine *Books In Print* and *Paperbound Books in Print*, plus the latest edition of *Forthcoming Books* to see if there are potentially competitive works.

☐ Read the competitive works in print.

☐ Ask yourself what makes your idea significantly different or better than the competition. These distinctions become your primary selling points. You need at least one major distinction between your idea and the competition for it to be saleable.

Proposal Mechanics

Most book proposals range from 15 to 30 pages. These proposals are always 100 percent typo-free with generous margins. Sometimes the proposals are double-spaced and other times they are single-spaced. The proposal takes many forms and the writer inevitably dictates the shape of the proposal. The common elements include:

☐ Overview. This area could be the most important part of your proposal and should be 1 to 3 pages long. In clear and succinct style it covers: What is the book about? Why the book is important, useful and necessary? Who is the audience? Who will buy this book? What makes the book different or better than any other book on this subject? What is the book's marketing handle? Each one of these is a 20 word or less description. What can you do to help the book in terms of promotion?

☐ Chapter Summaries. These summaries are an outline of the book. They can be as long as you desire but no less than 150 words for each chapter. Select the format that works best for you—i.e., outline, narrative, bulleted list of key points, etc.

☐ Sample Chapters. You will need at least one sample chapter and probably two or three (if a chapter is less than ten pages). These chapters should give the reader a strong sense of the book's tone and style. Many editors read the sample first so make sure you show your best work.

☐ About the Author. Don't be shy. Of everyone in the world, why should the editor give you this project? Specifically show how you are the most qualified individual for this project. The publisher is investing thousands of dollars in production costs for your adult nonfiction book title. Show your worth in this section.

☐ The Competition. Everyone believes their book is unique. It's not, so detail what other titles would be in direct competition.

☐ Manuscript Delivery and Length

☐ Promotion/Special Markets/Volume Buy Backs (anything over 5,000 copies)

Appendix C

The Thomas Nelson Guide to Writing a Winning Book Proposal

by Michael S. Hyatt

Even if you have previously had a book published you'll find tremendous value in preparing a formal book proposal. It will go a long way toward helping you to clarify your own thinking about the subject before you begin the actual writing process.

If there's one thing a publisher hates to see, it's a manuscript. Surprised? Most authors are. The fact is that publishers return most manuscripts to the author without ever having read them. Publishers simply do not have the time or staff to wade through the enormous number of manuscripts they receive from hopeful authors.

What a publisher really wants is a *book proposal*. Although you should include at least two sample chapters in your proposal, you should not finish writing the *entire* manuscript until the acquiring editor has approved the book's basic premise and structure, and the publisher has accepted the project for publication.

At Thomas Nelson Publishers we strongly believe in the creative interaction between author and editor. Out of this process come the best manuscripts. You'll find that most other publishers feel this way, too. Consequently, we want to give the author as much input as early in the writing process as possible. A book proposal gives us that opportunity.

So then, how do you prepare a good book proposal? From our experience, in addition to a captivating cover letter, it needs to include four distinct elements (see fig. 1 below for a complete outline):

• Title Page

• Proposal Overview

Figure 1: Comlete Book Proposal Outline

Title Page

Proposal Overview

I. The Content
   A. Premise
   B. Unique Selling Proposition
   C. Overview
   D. Manuscript
      1. Manuscript Status
      2. Special Features
      3. Anticipated Manuscript Length
      4. Anticipated Manuscript Completion Date

II. The Market
   A. Demographic Description
   B. Psychographic Description
   C. Affinity Group
   D. Competition

III. The Author
   A. Background
   B. Previous Writing
   C. Personal Marketing

Chapter-by-Chapter Synopsis

Two Sample Chapters

- Chapter-by-Chapter Synopsis

- Two Sample Chapters

This kind of proposal will accomplish two things. First of all, it will help us better evaluate your book idea and decide whether or not we want to pursue the project further. Second, even if you have previously had a book published, you'll find tremendous value in preparing a formal book proposal. It will go a long way toward helping you to clarify your own thinking about the subject before you get too involved in the actual writing process.

In order to illustrate these principles, let's create a book proposal. Be sure to keep in mind, though, that this is only a hypothetical book proposal—an example. It is not an absolute formula to be followed blindly. (Also, if you want to write a *fiction* book proposal, the format will be slightly different.) Though all good proposals mirror its basic content, each bears its own distinctive flavor as well. Now with that in mind, let's get to work.

For the sake of illustration, let's assume that you are a Christian financial planner. Through the years, you've observed that many of your clients' financial problems are the result of never having received adequate training in money management during childhood. You're convinced that if Christian parents would do a better job of training in this area, it would spare them—and their children—a tremendous amount of grief later in life.

Because of your conviction, you've worked hard to train your own children. You've even developed a seminar around this theme and taught it in a few churches. The response has been overwhelmingly enthusiastic.

Before long, several of your friends encourage you to write a book on the subject. Initially, you're flattered, and soon you begin to give the idea serious consideration. But where do you start? A book is such an enormous project! And how do you go about getting it published? The answer to both questions is a written *book proposal*.

Before you actually begin writing a book, you have to decide two things: what you want to say, and to whom you want to say it. In other words, you must determine the book's *content* and identify the book's *audience*. Once you've determined these things, it's time to go to work on the book's title.

Create the Title Page

We can't overemphasize the importance of developing a strong, catchy title. If the editor isn't "hooked" by the title, he will never open your proposal to see what is inside. The purpose of the working title is to focus your thinking as you develop the book idea. The working title should clearly encapsulate the book's premise. It might state the promise to the reader if he reads the book. It might even state the consequences if he doesn't. Sometimes the title will also include a subtitle. Let's consider the hypothetical book we introduced. After a little work, you come up with the following working title:

Helping Your Children Become Financially Responsible

After a little more thought, you add the following subtitle:

What Every Parent Should Know

This title clearly encapsulates the book's premise and communicates the promise to the reader.

Once you've come up with a title you need to remember that a working title is just that: a working title. It's tentative. You may decide to revise it later. Sometimes, the publisher will want to revise it. In any event, its purpose now is simply to focus the development of your book idea and to clearly—and quickly—communicate your book's basic idea.

Type the title neatly centered on one page. You should enter the subtitle on a separate line, directly under the title. Also, type the date you are submitting the proposal. Finally, type your name, address, and phone numbers near the bottom of the page. If you want, you can add an e-mail address (see fig. 2 on p. 158).

Write a Proposal Overview

The proposal overview consists of three distinct sections:
• The Content (What is the book about?)
• The Market (Who will buy this book?)
• The Author (Why are you the best possible author for this book?)

It should be no more than three to five single-spaced pages in length (see fig. 3-7, beginning on p. 160, for an example).

1. The Content

Once an editor flips past the title page, he then wants to know what the book is about. You can best communicate this by stating the book's premise, setting forth a few other details about your book.

Premise. The premise is a two- or three-sentence statement of the book's basic concept or thesis. Usually, it identifies the need and then proposes a solution. Let's return to the hypothetical book. What's the need you're trying to address? Isn't it the lack of training in money management that children are receiving from their parents? Or, to turn it around a bit, isn't it the failure of parents to teach their children how to become financially responsible that concerns you? After a little work, you come up with the following premise:

> Most children will leave their homes upon graduation from high school with little—if any—training in money management. As a result, they are likely to experience many years of struggle and frustration. The purpose of this book is to equip parents to teach their children the attitudes, principles and skills they need in order

to enjoy a life free of financial hassle and heartache.

Not bad. You've identified the problem, and you've said exactly what the book will do to solve it. And you've done it in three sentences! Developing a good premise is one of the most difficult challenges of good writing. It is, however, absolutely vital. Without it, your writing will lack clarity and focus. With it, your writing is more likely to be strong and forceful. It is well worth investing the time

Figure 2: Sample Title Page

A Book Proposal

**HELPING YOUR CHILDREN
BECOME FINACIALLY RESPONSIBLE**

What Every Parent Should Know

May 3, 1999

Submitted by
Frank B Slyer
2021 Lancaster Pike
Nashville, TN 37012

Office: (615) 242-1901
Home: (615) 791-2231

E-mail: fsalyer@spry.net

necessary to write a strong premise.

Unique Selling Proposition. Now that you have a premise, you need to focus on how the reader will benefit from reading your book. This is what publishers often refer to as the book's "take away" value—what the reader can expect to "take away" after reading the book. It is sometimes referred to as the book's *unique selling proposition*, or USP. This proposition clearly identifies what the reader will gain by reading the book (i.e., the book's *benefits*) and how the book will deliver it (i.e., the book's *features*). The simplest way to arrive at a solid USP is to complete this sentence (fill in the information between the brackets):

If consumers in the target market purchase and read [name of book], then they will [list the book's benefits], because the book will [list the book's features].

Now let's turn to our hypothetical book project, and create a compelling USP:

If consumers in the target market purchase and read Helping Your Children Become Financially Responsible,

Then they will:

- Understand what's at stake in the financial training of their children.
- Be able to pass on the most important attitudes, principles, and skills children must acquire before they can gain mastery over the money.
- Learn effective ways of communicating to children about money—with examples and metaphors children can understand.

Because the book will:

- Provide specific examples of parents who have succeeded.
- Outline a simple technique for money management.
- Build parents' confidence in their ability to teach their own children.

Figure 3: Sample Proposal Overview

PROPOSAL OVERVIEW

**HELPING YOUR CHILDREN
BECOME FINANCIALLY RESPONSIBLE**

What Every Parent Should Know

Frank B. Salyer

I. THE CONTENT

A. Premise
Most children will leave their home upon graduation from high school with little-if any-training in money management. As a result, they are likely to experience many years of struggle and frustration. The purpose of this book is to equip parents to teach their children the attitudes, principles, and skills they need in order to enjoy a life free of financial hassle and heartache.

B. Unique Selling Proposition
If consumers in the target market purchase and read Helping Your Children Become Financially Responsible,

Then they will:
• Understand what's at stake in the financial training of their children.
• Be able to pass on the most important attitudes, principles, and skills children must acquire before they can gain mastery over money.
• Learn Effective ways of communicating to children about money--with examples and metaphors children can understand

Because the book will:
• Provide specific examples of parents who have succeeded.

1

This kind of unique selling proposition clearly communicates to the editor reviewing your proposal that you know what you want the reader to get out of the book.

Overview. Once you have a solid premise and a clearly stated USP, you need to amplify them through the development of a general outline. At this point, you don't need a detailed, chapter-by-chapter synopsis (this will come later). You just need to be able to communicate the book's overall flow. Your goal is to give the editor reviewing your proposal the "big picture."

As a general rule, a nonfiction book should include at least three sections:

(1) description of the problem or need,

(2) presentation of the solution, and

(3) amplification of the solution through concrete applications.

As you develop the proposal for *Helping Your Children become Financially Responsible*, you need to identify the major sections. After looking back through your seminar notes, you come up with five:

- Part I: The Road to Frustration and Misery
- Part II: Five Attitudes Your Children Must Acquire
- Part III: Five Principles Your Children Must Learn
- Part IV: Three Skills Your Children Must Master
- Part V: The Envelope System of Cash Management

Of course you will also need an introduction and a conclusion. But the three basic parts are there: Part I will describe the problem or need, Parts II–IV will present the solution, and Part V will amplify the solution through a concrete application. Now that you have the major sections, you need to add a brief annotation to each, explaining in general terms what you intend to cover (again, see Figures 4 and 5).

Manuscript. Under this section, you need to cover the other details related to the manuscript. These would include the following:

1. Manuscript status: Where does the manuscript stand? Have you begun writing? How many chapters are finished?

2. Special features: Are there charts, graphs, tables, illustrations, photographs, etc.?

3. Anticipated number of manuscript pages or words: Generally speaking, each chapter should run between eighteen and twenty-two double-spaced manuscript pages and should be typed in a pica (12-

pitch) font. In order to arrive at the approximate length of the manuscript, simply multiply the number of chapters by what you think will be your average number of pages per chapter. If you prefer, you can also state the length of the manuscript in number of words. Depending on the font you use, the typical double-spaced manuscript page will contain approximately 250 words. Most modern "word processors" have a word count feature that will automatically give you a total.

4. Anticipated manuscript completion date: When do you anticipate completing the manuscript? In other words, when will it be ready to submit to your editor? You might want to set a goal of so many pages or words per day, week, or month. Make sure you set a realistic date.

2. The Market

Once you've determined the book's content, it's time to identify the book's audience. To a large degree, you've already done this, especially in developing the premise. However, in this part of the proposal, you need to be more specific. A good definition of the audience includes both its characteristics and its motivation. Let's look at these one at a time.

Characteristics. This is sometimes called the demographic description. The term *demographics* refers to the external, objective characteristics of your audience. It includes such things as gender, age, education-level, socio-economic status, geographic location (if any), religious affiliations, and so forth. In other words, you must determine if the book is for men, women, or both. Is it for Christians or a more general audience (Christians and non-Christians)? What is the reader's average age, income, political affiliation, theological orientation, and educational background? Try to describe the characteristics of the typical prospect. Let's take another look at our hypothetical book, *Helping Your Children Become Financially Responsible*. The first thing you'll want to consider is the kind of people who have

Figure 4: Sample Proposal Overview (continued)

Proposal Overview   Frank B. Salyer

- Outline a simple but effective technique for money management.
- Build parents' confidence in their ability to teach their own children.

C.   Overview
The manuscript is divided into five distinct parts:

1.   Part I: The Road to Frustration and Misery. Many adults suffer significant
     financial problems and heartache. Much of the pain is the direct result of
     never having been taught the simple principles of money management.
     Parents have within their power the ability to alleviate this pain. To do so,
     they must teach their children the right attitudes, principals, and skills.

2.   Part II: Five Attitudes Your Children Must Acquire.
     If children are to experience success in money man- agement later in life, they
     must first acquire the proper attitudes. Five of these provide a solid foundation
     for lasting financial peace: diligence, thrift, faithfulness, patience, and generosi-
     ty. A chapter will be devoted to each attitude.

3.   Part III: Five Principles Your Children Must Learn.
     The principles of money management are quite simple.
     There are five.
     - God owns it all.
     - You are His steward, responsible to Him.
     - Spend less than you make.
     - Pay God first, yourself second, and everyone else last.
     - Debt is dumb.
     A chapter will be devoted to each principle.

4.   Part IV: Three Skills Your Children Must Master. In addition to nurturing the
     proper attitudes and teaching the correct principles, a parent must also
     train children in three essential skills:

2

already shown an interest in your message. (If you haven't delivered the message orally, you'll have to describe the kind of people you *think* would be interested.) After jotting a few ideas down on paper, you come up with the following demographic description:

The audience for this book will be middle- to upper-middle-class Christian parents with at least a high school education who have children ages five through fifteen.

Figure 5: Sample Proposal Overview (continued)

Proposal Overview   Frank B. Salyer

- Developing a budget
- Managing a checkbook
- Making wise financial decisions

Again, a chapter will be devoted to each skill

5. Part V: The Envelope System of Cash Management. One of the most simple, easy-to-administer financial tools is the envelope system of cash management. Parents will be encouraged to adopt this system in managing their own finances and they will then be given a scaled-down version of it for their own children. A complete chapter-by-chapter synopsis is attached, giving a more detailed overview of the manuscript.

D. Manuscript

1. Manuscript status: Two chapters are completed (both are attached to this proposal as sample chapters).
2. Special Features: The manuscript will include various tables and charts, designed to graphically communicate important information in an easy-to-understand format. It will also include questions for discussion at the end of each chapter so the book can be used in small group study.
3. Anticipated manuscript length: 75,000 words (240 double-spaced, manuscript pages).
4. Anticipated manuscript completion date: Approximately three months after receiving a commitment from a publisher.

II. THE MARKET

A. Characteristics

The audience for this book will be middle- to upper-middle class Christian parents with at least a high school education who have children ages five through fifteen.

3

All you need now is a psychographic description to put "meat on the bones." In other words, you need to make your description three-dimensional.

Motivations. This is sometimes called the *psychographic* description. The term psychographics refers to the study of the motivations that lead people to consider your product and ultimately purchase it. While demographics involve the external, objective characteristics of your audience, psychographics involve the internal, subjective characteristics of your audience. Demographics tells you *who* and psychographics tells you *why*. For example, why would the reader want to buy your book? What are his frustrations? What motivates him? What does he expect to get out of the book?

Again, let's look at our hypothetical book. What needs and frustrations are characteristic of the target audience? You've already said that the child has a need to learn money management. But the child is not going to be the one buying the book; his parents are. What are their needs? After a little thought you come up with this:

> The audience for this book is made up of parents who have experienced frustration in their own lives as it relates to money management and, because they love their children, would like to spare them the same grief.

Now by combining these two definitions—the demographic and the psychographic—you will give the publisher a concrete idea of the audience you have in mind. But just as important, it will be an immense help to you as you begin writing the book. Specifically, it will guide you in your selection of appropriate vocabulary and illustrations.

Affinity Groups. The term *affinity* refers to "natural attraction or feeling of kinship." An affinity group is a body of people who will likely have some attraction to your book based on their behavioral history. Generally, you will think of and list several affinity groups. For example, if you were writing a book on marriage, a natural affinity group would be *Focus on the Family* radio listeners. If you were writing a book on starting a new business, a possible affinity group would be subscribers to *Income Opportunities* magazine.

Now consider our hypothetical book. What groups of people will likely be attracted to your message? After a little thought, you come up with the following:

- Listeners of Larry Burkett's *Money Management* radio show.
- Listeners of Dave Ramsey's *Financial Peace* radio show.

- Listeners of James Dobson's *Focus on the Family* radio show.
- Subscribers of *Money* magazine.
- Subscribers of *Parenting* magazine.
- Readers of financial books.
- People who have a professional relationship with a stockbroker.
- People who have a professional relationship with a financial planner.
- Financial counselors.

Notice that each group listed is identified by objective behavior. These are groups that (a) will be most likely to respond positively to your book's message and (b) the publisher can get to via one marketing vehicle or another.

Competition. Before you commit a great deal of time and energy to writing a book, you need to know what else is available. Why waste your time writing a book that has already been written? As Dawson Trotman, the founder of the Navigators, used to say, "Don't do anything that others can do or will do when there is so much of importance to be done that others cannot or will not do."

You may need to go to a bookstore and simply browse the shelves for books that address your subject or are in some way similar to the one you are proposing. Or you may want to flip through several current catalogs of the major publishers. It might even be a good idea to scan the subject and title listings in *Books in Print.*

The issue here is twofold:
1. Is there a proven market for this kind of book, and if so,
2. How does this book differ from other books like it?
   Differentiating your book from others is critically important.

Now that you've described the book and its audience, you need to take a little time and help the publisher get acquainted with you, the author.

3. The Author

Assuming the editor is interested in the content and believes that there might, in fact, be a market, the next thing he wants to know is why you are qualified to write it and what you are willing to do to help promote it.

Background. Describe your background, particularly as it relates to the subject of your book. Tell the publisher why you feel you are qualified to write the book. You may want to include a brief resume.

Figure 6: Sample Proposal Overview (continued)

Proposal Overview   *Frank B. Salyer*

B. Motivations
    The audience for this book is made up of parents who have experienced frustration in their own lives as it relates to money management and, because they love their children, would like to spare them the same grief.

C. Affinity Groups

    1. Listeners of Larry Burkett's *Money Management* radio show.
    2. Listeners of Dave Ramsey's *Financial Peace* radio show.
    3. Listeners of James Dobson's *Focus on the Family* radio show.
    4. Subscribers of *Money* magazine.
    5. Subscribers of *Parenting* magazine.
    6. Readers of financial books.
    7. People who have a professional relationship with a stockbroker.
    8. People who have a professional relationship with a financial planner.
    9. Financial counselors.

D. Competition
    I have not found a single book on this topic from either a secular or Christian perspective.

III. The Author

A. Background
    I have a B.A. in accounting from Michigan State University (1978) and an M.B.A. from Vanderbilt in Nashville. When I graduated from Vanderbilt in 1980, I went to work for Arthur Anderson where I worked for ten years. In 1990 I started my own financial planning business. I presently have thirty-five employees and 250 clients.

4

Your academic credentials may be important, but you may have other qualifications that are just as relevant. If so, be sure to mention them.

Previous Writing. Tell the publisher about your previous writing. Have you written a book or magazine article before? If so, what was it, who published it, and how did it do? Let the publisher know that samples of your written work are available upon request.

If you've never written before, that's fine, too; there's a first time for everyone. Just make sure you give specific reasons why you are the person to write the book.

Personal Marketing. A publisher cannot possibly do everything necessary to make your book successful. And most won't even try. Increasingly, publishers want to know what *you* can do to help promote the book. Consider the following:

- What important contacts do you have that might be willing to endorse the book?

- Are you presently speaking on the subject matter contained in the book? Are you willing to speak more? How many times per year? In what types of venues (e.g., churches, conferences, corporate seminars, etc.)?

- Are you planning to write articles based on the book?

- Would you be willing to create a Web site?

- Do you have any regular media opportunities? Television or radio appearances? Even a regular show?

Develop a Chapter-by-Chapter Synopsis
The purpose of a chapter-by-chapter synopsis or annotated out-

Figure 7: Sample Proposal Overview (continued)

Proposal Overview   *Frank B. Salyer*

B.   Previous Writing
     I have begun publishing a monthly newsletter as a result of interest
     expressed at my seminars (copies available upon request). I have also
     had one article published in *Christian Parenting* magazine. I've never
     written a book, but I think I would work well with an editor.

C. Personal Marketing

     I have developed a seminar with the same title as the proposed book. I have
     taught it in eleven churches and am willing to teach two seminars per month
     as a means of promoting the book.

     I will aggressively promote the book in my newsletter. I currently mail it to
     4,500 people, and the list is growing at the rate of about 500 per month.

     In addition, the Morning Show on Channel 5 television here in Nashville did
     an interview with me and a feature on my seminar. I received numerous pos-
     itive comments following my appearance and also received seventy-five let-
     ters.

5

line is to give you (and the editor) an overview of the book's structure. It should include section titles, chapter titles, and a two-or
three-sentence description under each chapter title of what will be
covered in that particular chapter (see Figure 8 on p. 170). In addition, this will convince the editor that you know where you are
going—and how you are going to get there.

You should pay particular attention to chapter titles. Like the
book's overall title, each chapter title must be interesting and intrigu-

Figure 8: Sample Proposal Overview (continued)

CHAPTER-BY-CHAPTER SYNOPSIS

**HELPING YOUR CHILDREN
BECOME FINANCIALLY RESPONSIBLE**

What Every Parent Should Know

Frank B. Salyer

PART ONE: THE ROAD TO FRUSTRATION AND MISERY

Chapter 1:   A Rude Awakening

This chapter will open with the story of Bill, a young Christian and recent college graduate who finds himself in deep trouble because of his inability to manage his own money. Bill is not alone. According to a recent *USA Today* poll, most Americans find themselves in the same boat. The inability to manage money leads to all kinds of suffering and frustration. In fact, most Americans are broke by age sixty-five and dependent on the generosity of their own families or the resources of the federal government.

Chapter 2:   Dropping the Baton

This chapter will open with the true story of an Olympic relay race—the team would have won, but the baton was dropped in the pass to the last runner. God gives parents the responsibility to teach and train their children. This responsibility is comprehensive; parents are to equip their children for life (see Deut. 6:4-9 and Prov. 22:6) and this includes the management of money.

Chapter 3:   Back to the Drawing Board

This chapter will open with the story of Don and Martha, two parents who did things right. They taught their own children how to manage

1

ing. In today's environment, the mass media have negatively affected the attention span of the reading public. People rarely read a book in one sitting. Every time they pick the book back up, the next chapter title has to convince them to keep reading. Therefore, it is extremely important that your chapter titles "pull" the reader back into the book.

Write Two Sample Chapters

If you've done your work well, the editor is now genuinely inter-

ested in your
proposal. There is only one question remaining: Can this author really write? The only way to demonstrate this is to include two sample chapters (see fig. 9 below). These chapters in the book don't have to be the first two in the book; and they don't even have to be consecutive. But they must be *good*. This is your audition for the publishing company and everything must go without a hitch.

I don't have space to tell you everything you need to know about

Figure 9: Sample Chapter

SAMPLE CHAPTER

CHAPTER ONE
A RUDE AWAKENING

Bill dropped his head into his hands. He rubbed his eyes and stared back at his computer in disbelief. the numbers were still the same. His checkbook was overdrawn and he still had several bills overdue. how in the world had he gotten into this mess?

It has all begun so innocently. Bill grew up in a stable, middle-class home. His father sold life insurance and his mother had stayed home to raise Bill and his two sisters. His parents didn't talk about money much, except their frequent comments that there was never enough of it to go around. Nevertheless, he never seemed to be in serious want. He worked several odd jobs growing up but was always free to spend the money as he wished. In his high school years, he spent most of it on his favorite hobby: restoring a 1955 Chevy to near-factory condition.

Like most of his friends, Bill went immediately from high school to college. He learned many things while at the university, but no one ever taught him the fine art of financial management. Amazingly, since his dad had paid for college, he never seemed to miss it. Until now.

When Bill graduated, he was immediately offered a job as a civil engineer. Soon, without his even asking, preapproved

1

writing, but here are a few quick pointers:

- Each chapter should be at least eighteen and no more than twenty-two double-spaced pages (approximately 9,000 to 15,000 words.)

- Begin each chapter with an attention-getting anecdote. Readers love stories, and there is no better way to pull the reader into the content of your chapter than with one.

- Break up the chapter using subheads. A good rule of thumb is to use at least one subhead every two pages.

- If possible, also include an anecdote or illustration somewhere under each subhead.

- Use active voice whenever possible. If you don't know the difference between active and passive voice, get a good grammar book and spend some time studying it.

- Carefully check the spelling and grammar of each chapter. Your word processor will likely give you a good start. But if these areas aren't your strong suit, hire a copy editor who can do it for you. This will cost you a little money, but it will be well worth the investment.

A Few Words of Caution

Remember, your proposal may be the only opportunity you will have to sell yourself and your concept to the publisher. Make every word count. Make certain that you come across well. First impressions make for lasting impressions. Therefore, take careful note of the following do's and don'ts:

- Do be polite, respectful, and friendly; don't make demands or launch into diatribes.
- Do make your proposal stylistically lucid, clear, and direct;

don't write with lurid ornateness, showing off your volu-
minous vocabulary.

- Do make certain that the proposal is neatly typed and sys-
tematically organized; don't send the publisher a faded
printout from a second-rate dot-matrix printer, a shoebox
of scraps, or a collection of random notes you've accumu-
lated over the last ten years.

- Do make sure all your facts and figures, names and dates,
people and places, are accurately noted; don't force the
publisher to sift the wheat from the chaff.

- Do engage in a little market research, sending your proposal
only to publishers whose backlist and editorial objectives
match the predisposition of your project; don't simply mail
out a query to every book house listed in the latest edition
of *Writer's Market*. Also don't send simultaneous submissions to any house unless you note this in a cover letter.

Conclusion

Preparing a book proposal like the one outlined here will require
a considerable investment of time and thought on your part.
However, this kind of investment will pay substantial dividends later when you begin the actual process of writing. More important,
perhaps, it will go a long way toward actually improving your
chances of getting published. Who knows? The next book you read
may be your own!

*Michael S. Hyatt is President of Thomas Nelson Publishers, Inc., the
largest Christian publishing company in the world and the ninth largest
publishing company of any kind. Thomas Nelson Publishers is publicly-
traded on the New York Stock Exchange under the symbol TNM. Mike
has worked at the company for a total of nine years. He has been
involved in the publishing industry more than twenty-five years. Prior
to coming to Thomas Nelson, he was a partner in the literary agency of*

Wolgemuth & Hyatt, Inc. He is the author of four books, including The Millennium Bug, *which was on the New York Times Business Bestseller list for seven consecutive months. His latest book is entitled* Invasion of Privacy: How to Protect Yourself in the Digital Age. *Michael and his wife, Gail, have been married for twenty-six years and have five daughters and one granddaughter. They live outside Nashville, Tennessee.*

© 1998 Michael S. Hyatt
Used with permission of the author

Appendix D

Strategies for a Six-Figure Advance

One of the more interesting free documents that I have read recently about proposals is called *Strategies for a Six Figure Book Advance*. This short document studies 20 books that sold for over $100K since July 2002. Mahesh Grossman compiled the material in this document. I can't distribute this work because it's not mine but you can get it by going to this website: http://snipurl.com/wabty.

The site contains a simple form for your email address and first name. You will receive the report automatically after entering your address. In addition, this form signs you for a twice monthly newsletter (you can unsubscribe at any time). I've found this newsletter another valuable and free resource.

After you get this *Strategies for a Six Figure Book Advance* document, take the time to study the resource to learn what the individuals did or wrote about to achieve this type of success. There are no guarantees in publishing that you can do the same, but you will learn something valuable about nonfiction proposals from the experience.

Appendix E

Agent List

Here's another great resource for any writer—and I can't distribute it since I didn't write it, but I can lead you to it. It's an eight page list of about 400 literary agents with their name, agency, address, phone number and in some cases a website. It is not comprehensive because when I looked at it for a few minutes I found a number of agents that are not on this list. You may find this resource valuable for you. You can get it at: http://snipurl.com/auths.

As with the previous appendix resource, you will need to enter your email address and first name into a form. In a few minutes, you will receive this list and be added to a newsletter list (you can unsubscribe at any time). This resource will give you some names and addresses of people to approach with your polished nonfiction book proposal.

Appendix F

Website Shortcuts

Throughout this book, I reference a number of different websites. Instead of listing long website addresses, I've used a web tool called SNIPURL (http://snipurl.com) and reduced each one to a short listing. Because SNIPURL is a free tool and outside of my personal control, I've listed both websites in this appendix to assure that you, the reader, can reach these websites. Each site was current and functional at the time this book went to press.

Introduction
http://snipurl.com/novel
http://www.amazon.com/exec/obidos/tg/detail/-/1582972567/web-pageforauthow/

How do you follow the trends in publishing?
Publisher's Weekly website
http://snipurl.com/pweek
http://www.publishersweekly.com/

Publisher's Lunch
http://snipurl.com/publunch
http://www.publishersmarketplace.com/lunch/free/

Book Publishing Statistics
http://snipurl.com/bkstat
http://parapub.com/statistics/

Publicize Your Book! (Secret 7)
http://snipurl.com/pubyb

http://www.amazon.com/exec/obidos/tg/detail/-/0399528636/web-pageforauthow/

Jenkins Book Group (Secret 7)
http://snipurl.com/jenkins
http://www.bookpublishing.com/about.htm?pg=cs

Beyond the Bookstore (Secret 7)
http://snipurl.com/btbks
http://www.amazon.com/exec/obidos/tg/detail/-/1594290024/web-pageforauthow

Jacqueline Marcel, Elder Rage article (Secret 10)
http://snipurl.com/Elder
http://www.pma-online.org/scripts/shownews.cfm?id=526

***Running On Ice* (Secret 10)**
http://snipurl.com/roivf
http://www.amazon.com/exec/obidos/tg/detail/-/156309911X/webpageforauthow/002-1545600-2996814

Join a Critique Group to Get Your Writing Moving
http://snipurl.com/criti (Secret 12)
http://www.right-writing.com/critique.html

The Safest Way To Search For An Agent
http://snipurl.com/safest (Secret 17)
http://www.right-writing.com/published-safest.html

The First Five Pages by Noah Lukeman (Secret 17)
http://snipurl.com/Firstfive
http://www.amazon.com/exec/obidos/tg/detail/-

/068485743X/qid%3D1101398032/webpageforauthow/002-
1545600-2996814

**Literary Agents, A Writer's Introduction by John F. Baker (Secret
17)**
http://snipurl.com/literary
http://www.amazon.com/exec/obidos/tg/detail/-/0028617401/web-
pageforauthow/

**Association of Author Representatives Frequently Asked Questions
(Secret 17)**
http://snipurl.com/aarfaq
http://www.aar-online.org/faq.html

**Which Conferences Are Worth It? article on Right-Writing.com
(Secret 19)**
http://snipurl.com/conferences
http://www.right-writing.com/conferences.html

Write A Book Today website (Appendix D)
http://snipurl.com/wabty
http://www.writeabooktoday.com

Author Secrets .com website (Appendix E)
http://snipurl.com/auths
http://www.authorsecrets.com

Appendix G

12 Maxims for Any Writer

The final appendix for this book will again remind you of some of my operating principles as a writer and editor throughout my career. I hope as much as the 21 secrets in this book, these maxims will aid you in your overall writing career.

1. Never forget the impact of your words—positive or negative. Most days, I feel the pressure of motivation to make money as a freelancer. I've got bills and obligations which demand payment. Yet if you are so money-driven that you never make any decisions about your writing except ones which are motivated from finances, it will be difficult for you to advance in nonfiction or whatever category you choose. Don't get me wrong. I want to be fairly compensated for my work but I also want to enjoy my work and what I do day in and day out. You need to be conscious of your motivation behind your writing and let that drive your daily efforts.

2. Never forget your writing is a privilege and a business—so seek to maintain balance. Too many writers hesitate to ask for their materials or for a decision about a query or proposal. They send it out once or twice, then it's rejected and they don't properly market.

3. Celebrate your writing successes. Never lose the wonder of the opportunity. At another conference I attended—a secular writing conference in Southern California—I was fascinated by a secular novelist and his message. While waiting to ask him a question after the session, I turned to another person and asked if she had taken this instructor's writing class. The woman puffed up her face in disgust and replied, "No, I'm a published author." Just because our material is printed in magazines or books, it should not build us up in pride. Believe me, sometimes it's difficult but as writers we need to keep things in balance, especially when it comes to nonfiction books.

4. Believe in the quality of your work and the value of your message. Surprises always happen. I work hard at my craft and perseverance is a key factor. Don't get me wrong but I love to receive my material in print. It's a surprise and a special blessing. It's the new box of books hot off the press or the magazine article in a missionary publication. I marvel at the grace in my life. I'd encourage you to absorb the same attitude no matter how many books you publish.

5. Expect to serve an apprenticeship. It's a false expectation to go from nothing to book contracts. Everyone is expected to move through the ranks of this business. It takes diligence and perseverance to succeed.

6. Learn all you can from every possible source. If you approach life in this fashion, you will find that you can learn from a multitude of sources.

7. Act wisely and thoughtfully. Haste usually makes waste.

8. Never resist rewriting. Your words are not etched in stone.

9. Never resist editing. Again, your words are not etched in stone.

10. When you receive advice about your writing, learn to evaluate it critically. Sometimes you will get advice from a fellow writer or a family member and it doesn't "feel" like something you should take. Follow that instinct.

11. Treat editors as the coach on your team. They know their audience, so respect their counsel and only reject it with good reason.

12. Never rest on your laurels. Be looking for your next opportunity. I've discovered that writing opportunities abound—particularly when I'm actively looking for them.

Vital Resources for the Christian Writer!

Check out these great tools at **www.writenowpublications.com**
or use the handy order form on the back of
this page to order these books directly!

ORDER FORM

Qty	Title	Price	Total
	Book Proposals that Sell *W. Terry Whalin*	$14.00	
	A Complete Guide to Christian Writing and Speaking — *Susan Osborn, Editor*	$15.00	
	A Complete Guide to Writing for Publication *Susan Osborn*	$15.00	
	How to Write and Sell a Christian Novel *Gilbert Morris*	$12.00	
	An Introduction to Christian Writing *Ethel Herr*	$17.00	
	Just Write *Susan Osborn*	$12.00	
	Write His Answer *Marlene Bagnull*	$14.00	
	You Can Market Your Book *Carmen Leal*	$15.00	
		Subtotal	
		+ Shipping and Handling*	
		Total	

* Shipping and Handling: Add $4.00 shipping and handling for the first book and $1.00 for each additional book.

Purchase these books from your local bookstore or contact:

Write Now Publications
5501 N. 7th Ave., #502
Phonix, AZ 85013

800-931-BOOK (2665)

www.writenowpublications.com